HIGHLAND DAYS

Highland Days

Tom Weir

*with thirty-one photographs
by the author*

GORDON WRIGHT PUBLISHING
25 MAYFIELD ROAD, EDINBURGH EH9 2NQ
SCOTLAND

British Library Cataloguing in Publication Data

Weir, Tom
 Highland days.
 1. Mountaineering—Scotland
 I. Title
 796.5′22′0924   GV199.44.G72S27

 ISBN 0-903065-51-7

Typeset by Jo Kennedy, Edinburgh
Printed and bound by Billing & Sons Ltd, Worcester

Nothing that can come to me now can equal those
shining days when the bloom was on the grapes of
discovery and every ramble was a radiant adventure
in a new-created world.

EDWARD A. ARMSTRONG
(Birds of the Grey Wind)

Acknowledgements

With deep felt thanks to Peter Currie who encouraged
me to write and to Robert Anderson who drew the maps.

Contents

Preface

This is a new edition of Tom Weir's first book, completed in 1946 and published in 1948, and it is clear by the interest shown and the scarcity of secondhand copies that there is a real demand for its reissue.

Tom Weir has achieved his early ambition to be a writer and explorer and today he is universally respected in both those fields. Tom Weir is of the folk, and his sensible and sensitive comments on the Scottish landscape and all who live there are warmly enjoyed everywhere. In all my travels in Scotland, Tom's name always evokes affection and respect.

The information in this book is both dated and timeless. It is difficult for example, to know whether a particular expedition or climb was done when he was seventeen or thirty. The mountains and the weather have not changed. His love of the game is wholly stable. And time, to most of us in memory, is not a matter of duration measured by the ticking of a clock; it is a matter of intensity.

Tom writes vividly of what happened. He deals in a rush of words about something which happened to him; which he had fiercely dreamed of doing – exploring mountain country. I use the word 'fiercely' by careful choice. It is as I see him: his eyes and face, when he is intent on a rock face; lifting his binoculars to watch an eagle; or telling me of something he is going to write. He is, above most men I've known, a man of strong intent and tenacity. But all these characteristics—not always those of peace—are devoted to the beauty and life of our countryside and its meaning to the human part of life.

Highland Days is fundamentally an innocent book. That was what I thought when I first read it nearly forty years ago, and had known Tom only a few years. We shared the same background, in the north of Glasgow, in sight of the Campsie Hills, true mountains to us, and our discovery of them on very long walks, mostly without money, were genuine explorations and escapes from the tenements where we lived.

By the time Tom had written this book my professional career had led me into certain kinds of public responsibilities and taught me how our environment had evolved – including mountain country, and about the thrust and counter thrust of town and country. When I talked to Tom about it, I found that he too had 'opened the books' as Jack London put it in his splendid book *Mark Eden*.

So I come back to why I use the word 'innocent'. *Highland Days* is really about Tom's own Garden of Eden, as it was in the beginning. His subsequent writing and broadcasts show his continuing growth of understanding of the need for what I once called 'the invisible web of administration' which, one day, our society may weave to protect the environment which nourishes us all. But behind any good administration there must be heard the shout of joy from the Garden; and this book is exactly that.

Prof. Sir Robert Grieve

Prologue

To be born in a town is not without its compensations. The smoke of Glasgow and the city's prison of drab tenements are themselves a driving force to escape, though we had never heard of escapism when, as youngsters in torn and patched breeks, with bottles of water and a "jeely piece" (a jelly sandwich for those who do not know), we went out to find the green places that are everywhere on the outskirts of our city.

We played games, climbed trees, collected rowan berries for our pea-shooters, "dooked" in the canal, but above all, I can recollect, it was a wonder for nature that moved us. To find a bird's nest was the most magic thing in life. Sometimes we carried the nests home with us, but we did not know any better. I scoured the Juvenile Library of Springburn for books to teach me bird biology. Thus I mounted a hobby horse which twenty years later I am still riding.

The bus to Campsie Glen used to race past our door. Campsie was the fabled land of great hills and extraordinary treasures. We could see the long ridge from high points in the district, and their bold, precipitous front had a fascination that had to be transmuted to action. An Easter holiday, and three urchins with various sacks tied round them might have been seen setting out on foot for this magic country. One of us was deficient of a blanket, but in lieu he had two sugar bags which served as a double-layer sleeping-bag. Our tent was a home-made affair of patch-sheets.

The walk seemed endless, but what adventurers we were, camped that night by a little burn on the summit of the wild moor that sweeps to Fintry! We explored gorges, forced a way up unknown rivers, and our discoveries had all the thrills of Stanley or Livingstone in them. I came back from that week-end with a yearning for green places that would not be denied. Mountains and birds seemed the most important things in life.

The search for fulfilment in these things is the story of this book.

T. W.

1

A Reverie

...Why do I yield to that suggestion
Whose horrid image doth unfix my hair,
And make my seated heart knock at my ribs.
MACBETH

SITTING writing this in a guard-tent in the blazing heat of a
Belgian July I find it hard to believe that my memories are
thirteen years old.

"Is it thirteen years", I ask myself, "since I fearfully traced
out of Abraham's *British Mountain Climbs* dotted lines up the
face of Buachaille Etive Mór, and produced diagrams of likely
routes I could climb solo?" I was seventeen then.

Seventeen! Life consisted of weeks-ends and holidays. Week-
end camps by Loch Long and Loch Lomond; days on the old
"Ben" and the "Cobbler". How proud I felt after doing my first
real rock-climb: a schoolboy effort on the jammed block chimney
of Ben Narnain. That spring when the delights of Ben Lui and
Ben More were mine and the glamour of the unknown was over
every vista of jumbled peaks that opened out from the summits!
Those evenings on the Campsie Fells watching the sun set over
the Cowal Hills! My epic with Richie when we had gone exploring the length of Loch Etive, crossed over the Lairig Eilde and
gone over by the Blackwater to Kinlochleven! Then over Ben
Nevis and Aonach Beag and down across Rannoch! All too
vividly I recall the weight of our packs and the trembling of my
limbs in extreme fatigue. Richie told me that I had "the knock"
and carried my bag in addition to his own.

There was little doubt that I considered myself a first-class
climber thirteen years ago—hence the diagrams of Buachaille
Etive's face and my preoccupation with *British Mountain Climbs*.
The emancipated mountaineer was about to take a holiday! The
thought of going away on my own was the only damper, but it
did not weaken my resolution.

Then came a stroke of good fortune. New-found friends of mine, Matt Forrester and John MacNair, volunteered to join me for the week-end, so for the first three days I should have company. My luck had started.

What a wonderful first day to a holiday that was! Not for weather, which was showery, but for the sheer joy of being on the tops and coming back to a delightful camping spot we had walked far to find. Over a fire of bog pine we sang Gaelic songs and afterwards lay in the tent talking. It was the first time I had been out with real mountaineers and I felt proud to be in their company. Matt told us of a fellow he had met who believed in the "wee folk".

"Who are the wee folk?" I asked, for this was the first I had heard of them.

"D'you mean to say you have never heard of the wee folk?" said Matt incredulously.

I had to admit my ignorance.

John and Matt knew all about them. I was told how children used to be lost from the villages of Galloway, and of weird, unaccountable happenings amongst the hills; of haunted places where even to this day people will not venture. This was an aspect of hill-lore undreamed of by me. Then came "water kelpies" that bewitched the senses and spirited innocent people from their homes, never to be seen again.

Half-heartedly I expressed my disbelief. "The old folk-tales of the north are too full of these stories for them to be mere inventions," said the positive John.

"Now here is a queer thing," went on Matt. And I was told of a monster that dwells in a tarn high up on Ben Lawers. On moonlight nights it rises out of the water, its talons dripping blood. Round the mountain it prowls, moaning in an awful way. Matt told of a climber who had the temerity to camp by the lochan and who was found dead with a look of wild terror on his face. The disorder inside the tent told its own story.

"Do you believe these tales?" I asked. Matt and John thought there was something in them.

"Take the 'Ferlie Mhor' for instance," went on Matt. "If Professor Collie had the wind-up about the 'grey man' of the Cairngorms, there must be something in it. And more than one has seen it too, even in these times. It haunts Ben MacDhui.

Ghostly footsteps crunching out of the mist precede its visitations, then a horrible grey shape emerges. The sensation of fear is overpowering, they say, and old Collie didn't stop running till he got in to Aviemore!"

All too well I knew what unreasoned terror was. Terror of the dark when I was very young, then at a later stage terror of the "Banshee". A schoolboy companion had told me all about the latter, and for weeks after I heard its death wail in every sound that broke the night silence. I heard it in the hoisting of the family washing, in the screech of pulleys from the kitchen, and even in the squeaking of a door. Here was a new menace.

They went to sleep—I to dream.

I shall always remember the following day as one of the happiest of my life. In the early morning sunshine Ben Starav was a point of purple-blue, and we went to it up past Loch Dochart by a wild glen. Even now I can recall the Firth of Lorne and Duart Castle of Mull as it looked that afternoon thirteen years ago; see again the Crowberry Tower of Buachaille that sent our spirits soaring with desire; and in imagination I wander up that rocky ridge that took us over Glas Bheinn Mhór, Stob Coirean Albannaich and Meall Nan Eun. That was a day of living, of good company, and sunshine that sparkled as bright as memory.

Next day I saw them go back to Glasgow. They had to leave early, for we were camping off the beaten track and Bridge of Orchy was a fair walk. John told me afterwards I looked miserable as I said good-bye. I felt miserable—miserably lonely.

Stob Ghabhar was above me for climbing and without enthusiasm I started up it. At two thousand feet a grouse rising from the heather startled me out of my wits. The "creaking" of ptarmigan was an evil sound, and the echoing roar of mountain torrents rising and falling on the wind had a sinister threat that dinged my ears. Furtively I looked around, expecting to see the "wee folk" or worse closing in for a snatch. Once a hare started up from under my feet and I could have screamed for fear—I the emancipated mountaineer aged seventeen. Mist dropped round the peak as I gained the top, adding its mystery to an already mysterious enough universe, but I forced myself to traverse the tops.

It was dusk when I got back to camp, and raining. The spot I had thought so fine was now bleak and hostile; the glen I had thought so fine was as desolate and remote as Tibet. Unutterably lonely, with my head deep in my blanket, I tried to sleep. The chuckling of the burn was a conversation torturing my imagination by its variety of sounds. I felt like the victim in an Edgar Allan Poe tale.

But morning came—beautiful daylight! What matter if it was sullen and grey? I would get away to Buachaille Etive Mór and make one of these dotted lines a reality. I would prove myself to myself. With no regrets I left the glen for the old Glen Coe road and got a lift to Kingshouse. Two or three miles along I pitched my tent under the crags of the "Big Shepherd".

What a hope of choosing a route! It was pouring with rain, and the rocks disappeared black and slippery into clouds. Nevertheless, I did my duty and climbed my peak by an unknown rock route, returning on a compass course by the easy way to the *bealach*. I felt a new man when I got back to the tent. No symptoms of fear, at least superstitious fear, had bothered me at all on the peak. Route finding had occupied my thoughts, so it seemed to me that all this was just a matter of concentration. Confidently I cooked my supper and turned in to bed. But I was still awake in the darkness of the night, fighting a nameless terror. The doctrine of pure reason that had stood me in good stead all day was woefully insufficient now. With the dawn, I found sleep.

All that day it rained. I could have packed up my tent and camped beside a house which was near by, but my pride forbade it. I would beat this thing. My common sense told me I was just being stupid. There were no such things as supernatural beings! Why, as a boy I had climbed solo and even camped solo without any of my present miseries!

But I was saved further trouble, for that night, having a stroll in the glen, I met an acquaintance. He had walked up from Onich despite the rain and gladly accepted the offer of a berth in my tent. How glad I was of his company he never knew, for I was too ashamed of my fears to tell him.

Next day we climbed the "Little Shepherd", Buachaille Etive Beag, in a day of scudding mist, and I felt I had come alive again. The familiar joy of being on the tops was once again mine. That was the finish of my holiday and I came home with a skeleton in the rucksack.

Early autumn saw John and I in Torridon in glorious weather, among peaks of a splendour I had never dreamed of. By our camp fire beside our little tent we would yarn and sing when the climbing was over and the moon had risen high in the sky. My happiness was complete, and such stupid fears as I had once entertained just did not exist any longer. I determined to learn the secret of the same kind of happiness when I was by myself, for climbing companions are not always to hand. I had read too, what the late A. F. Mummery says about solitary climbers and wanted to reach that independence of mind and ability necessary to the solitary climber.

September of that same year I made good my resolution. Of all the supernatural stories I had been told, that inhabitant of the lochan on Ben Lawers was most vivid in my mind, so up there I decided to go. That wild look of terror on the dead climber's face haunted my imagination. Matt came with me for a couple of days, but I was left with a day and a half to storm my fear. My tent was pitched high on the Lochan na Lairig and the whole range of mountains was mine.

Darkness fell early and by candle-light I read *The Forsyte Saga*. I noted with satisfaction that my mind was on the book and not on the sighing of a monster. At eleven o'clock I blew out the candle and concentrated on sleep. Vague fears as of old began to assail and upset my reason before long. But I had made up my mind what was to be done. I got up and went outside. No more burying my head in the blankets.

My heart throbbing, I looked around. A fringe of gauzy cloud, a scarf of moon-tinted vapour against the shadowy summit of Ben Lawers banished the thought of anything else. The still beauty of everything made my stupid fears seem childish. I got back into bed, laughing at my credulity. I did not laugh for long, but at each recurrence of uneasiness I went outside again and banished it.

Often since then I have felt lonely on mountains. Often I have been conscious of an unknown presence, especially camping and sleeping out, a feeling impossible to explain and not at all unpleasant. But after Lochan na Lairig I did not go looking for "wee folk" and I did not find any.

2

An Epic

It was fourteen years ago on a Loch Lomond bus that I first met Richie. I was sixteen at the time and my ambition in life was to be an explorer. I had read everything about the Arctic and Antarctic that I could lay my hands on and here, for the first time, was a kindred spirit. I can see him now as I write, a quiet, rather grim-looking man with yellow hair going a bit thin on top. His quietness was noticeable, for the bus-load were singing their heads off after a successful Easter week-end.

He leaned across and asked me if I had been walking, for although dressed as a schoolboy complete with skull-cap—in order to get half-fare on the bus—I was carrying an army pack. I confessed my enthusiasm as is the way of youth, and he took me seriously. Indeed, he confessed to similar ambitions.

I did not expect to see him again, but by a coincidence met him later at Rowardennan one moonlight Saturday night as I searched the foreshore for a camping place. We shared the tent and got on famously. Richie seemed to know every part of the Scottish Highlands. He had been a cyclist and had just taken to walking and climbing.

He was unemployed and spent most of his time outdoors, going back to Glasgow from Tuesday to Thursday to sign his name at the Labour Exchange. Politics entered my life at this time too, for Richie was embittered against a government that had no work to offer, and rather than walk the streets he walked the hills. He was a plumber and in his kit he carried a few tools of his trade, so that he could pick up an odd penny by wee jobs such as repairing milk cans and so on.

He was a little chap, not more than five feet six in height, but very strong. Weight-lifting and wrestling were his hobbies, and I remember that week-end there was a health-and-strength club camping in the bay. We were sitting on the foreshore when a big chap, stripped to the waist and of magnificent physique,

See Central Highlands map, page 57.

6

offered to "pull" any one of the party. No one spoke and after a short silence Richie said he might have a try. It was a David-and-Goliath sort of tournament, but I have a vivid recollection of the big chap's shoulders being forced down on the gravel so mercilessly that blood streamed down his back. Later, when weight-lifting with boulders, Richie capped all their efforts by doing a "bent press" with an enormous stone!

That, then, was the man. As well as revolutionary ideas on politics, he had revolutionary ideas on walking. He wanted to do it the hard way, the explorer's way, across Scotland by the mountain-tops, self-supporting in food and sheltering where one could. This was what I wanted, and Richie had an idea for a tour, provided I could get my holiday when he was allowed off by the Labour Exchange.

It all worked out, and late one night a man and a boy might have been seen boarding the Oban train. Probably the watcher would even have permitted himself a laugh, for the boy, small for his age, was carrying a Bergan rucksack of huge bulk that reached far below its proper place in the small of his back. To counteract its weight he had to bend nearly double, the motion being as near turtle-like as makes no difference.

Taynuilt was our destination and in the grey of the morning we fortified ourselves with a meal. When I say "fortified", I mean "fortified"—at least as far as Richie was concerned. He prided himself on being a good trencherman. He was more than that. In amazement I watched our store of food dwindle as Richie "packed it away", to use his own expression. Our food was supposed to last a week, but I knew there and then that it would not.

Ben Cruachan, whose tops we were supposed to promenade over to Ben Starav, was in cloud. Also its slopes looked fearfully long and steep for our heavy bags, so we decided that, since there was nothing to be gained by going up into mist, we would go up the seldom visited west side of Loch Etive. There was a track marked on the map, but the toil of that rucksack made each step a separate effort of will.

I can remember little of that walk except a pair of dogs that Richie antagonized by swinging a stick at them and hissing like a cat. He antagonized all dogs in fact, so that I was in terror each time we came to a house. What I can remember is that evening at the head of Glen Etive. All the toil was worth while just to be ringed round by the great hills, rocky and green, and seamed with innumerable cataracts that filled the air with sound. How delightful to be free of the sack and to be at last "exploring"!

Morning saw us take to the hills in rain by a wild pass, the Lairig Eilde, which at length led into Glen Coe. An impression of cloudy gloom and fierce toppling crags remains distinct from the glen as I know it to-day. Under a rock we ate the last of our food and were joined by a tramp.

Richie was not flattered at being asked if I was his son, and answered rather sharply to the contrary. Prematurely thin on top myself at thirty I can understand how he felt at twenty-eight to be mistaken for the father of such a precocious youngster. I had many inward chuckles later as the same mistake was made time after time by people whom we met. At the time I thought Richie super-sensitive on the point.

Richie's interest in the tramp was more than passing, for he had a hankering to try the life himself, and he questioned the tattered-looking fellow on the technique of the craft. It was a mean sort of existence, of begging and labouring, and of model lodging-houses in the big towns when winter came. The tramp's last words were: "Keep off the game, it's only for down-and-outs like me." As he shambled down that bleak moor in his rags, purposeless and alone in an inhospitable world, I found my first romantic picture shattered. "What a life for ever," I thought.

It was afternoon now, and we climbed up a heathery hill-side, the north-enclosing face of the glen. We were *en route* for Loch Leven. What went wrong I do not know—our map was a motoring one three miles to the inch, so I suspect that had something to do with it—but for hours we crossed an expanse of heather and bog "God-forsaken and man-forsworn". At length a long slash of water gleamed. We thought it was Loch Leven but tasted its water to make sure. It was fresh and sweet, therefore not Loch Leven water. We scanned the map and decided it was the Blackwater.

It was on the shores of this loch that I was seized with a trembling of the lower limbs. I did not say anything but my weakness was apparent to Richie, for I was lagging behind. I had "the knock" he informed me, a complaint common among hard-pushing cyclists. Food was the only cure but we had none, so he bravely shouldered my pack in addition to his own and we pushed on. Late that night we camped at the foot of a huge, thundering waterfall, the biggest I had ever seen, and in my imagination now as tremendous as Niagara. We came far that day.

But Kinlochleven was not far off, and after a breakfastless start, we got there around midday. Richie bought the groceries while I went to a house for water. "Is it Tinkers?" she asked as she handed me the brimming can. We got the stove going behind an outhouse and, regardless of the curious townsfolk, had a meal which is an event in my memory.

A convenient bus took us to Fort William and that night saw us in the half-way hut on Ben Nevis. It was a beautiful evening and the silver lochs to the west and the massive peaks of the Mamores to the south enraptured us. All the charm that the Scottish hills have for me is conveyed in that fragment of memory. It is too indefinite to explain, but I can see a collection of giant hills and lochs probably more akin to the mountains of the moon than reality.

Right through the night people kept coming into the hut on their way to the top for the sunrise. It was cold up there wrapped in a solitary blanket and we were glad to get moving ourselves. Mist had crept down to us and up into a thickening gloom we climbed. Somehow I hoisted that pack to the top. Below us were the dripping wet crags of the wildest place I had ever seen.

Our plan was to traverse the mountain into the upper part of the glen, so we were not at all careful where we went down. Anyway we got entangled on the crags. I suspect we descended quite a bit of the north-east buttress for I have a fearful recollection of crying for help as I sought for handholds, while the weight of my bag nearly dragged me to perdition. The crags seemed to drop away sheer below us, yet we kept on going. Fate looked after us more kindly than we deserved, for we got down.

Richie was elated. "We'll climb Aonach Beag," he cried. We left the bags and seemed to float up it, so easy did it feel after our bag-hoisting efforts. There was nothing to see except dirt-scarred snow-beds, hard as ice, in the hollows. Actually I think it was Aonach Mór we climbed, but whatever it was we enjoyed it! How we bounded down that peak, whooping with delight at our achievements and the release from the bondage of the packs! There was something unutterably satisfying about these great green slopes seamed with wild mountain torrents and scattered with boulders.

We were soaked through, not relishing the prospect of camping, when a miracle in the shape of a little tin bothy at the junction of two rivers gave us the shelter we needed. It was cold on the concrete floor but we did not complain. The purring of the stove was cheery and we felt the warm glow of comradeship in us.

The rain still fell as we pushed down towards Loch Treig on the morning following. There was no track, the floor of the glen was sodden and the river in wild spate. At last with the rain running out of us we came to a lonely house, unfortunately on the wrong side of the river. We had an urge to get into a barn or shed, and maybe we could get a few eggs.

We surveyed the stepping-stones submerged by a swirling brown flood. I shall never forget that crossing. As a foot was lowered to reach a stone, the force of the river would sweep it aside, and the movement of the water tended to confuse the senses. Luckily they were flat stones, but in mid-stream I felt as isolated as a man all alone in a cobble in mid-Atlantic. I could see myself bobbing up and down in that brown rush to be flung in cataract into Loch Treig. But I got across safely.

The people of the house were friendly and gave us eggs and flour. We could use their barn if we wished, but they recommended our going on to Loch Ossian where a house had been put at the disposal of walkers and climbers. This was news to us so we pushed on. I will draw a veil over the short cut we tried to take to reach this house. Short cuts never pay on Rannoch, and when we at last stepped off that quaking bog on to a path that took us to the house, we were more than thankful.

The door was locked but we entered by a window. We felt we were expected. On a table stood a jar of almonds and raisins and there was an enormous store of firewood. Soon all our clothes were on the pulleys and a great fire was roaring up the chimney. Over it we made pancakes with our eggs and flour and Richie initiated me into the mysteries of French toast. That was a happy night. We sat in our birthday suits while our clothes steamed merrily above us. An abundance of blankets saw us warmly through the night. I learned afterwards that the building was called a Youth Hostel. This was my first experience of something that was to popularize the whole outdoor movement.

We had decided to go down to Rannoch and climb some peaks from there. At Corrour, next morning, a convenient train was standing in the tiny station, so we piled into it as there was no time to buy tickets. Its first stop was Crianlarich so our plans were spoiled. We walked along the railway line to near Tyndrum, and, as the weather was wet and cloudy, parked ourselves in a railway bothy, the key of which had been handily placed under a stone.

Richie was in a quarrelsome mood that night and told me off severely for "filthy habits" when I licked a blob of condensed milk off the edge of the tin after pouring some out. I explained that I had picked up the habit from him in the first instance, but he did not take it kindly.

The atmosphere was rather tense when we went to bed but Richie's temper was to find an outlet in the morning. We were awakened by a loud thundering on the door with an angry command to know, "Who the hell is in there?" Our fire had been seen. "Don't answer," said Richie. He drew on his trousers.

"Open up at once or I'll have the police on you," the voice shouted. "You have no business here at all."

Richie flung open the door, chin thrust out in a look of angry determination that would have daunted the boldest. "Who do you think you are talking to?" His voice was quiet.

The man continued to shout. "Listen," said Richie. "Get the police. Get who you like but don't stand there shouting at me. I'll not have it. Get out!" He took a step towards the man. The man fled.

"Now for a quick getaway," said Richie. We made off up the slope of Ben Lui, traversed its misty top, and dropped into Glen Falloch. Richie's bad temper had gone, so I was grateful to that railwayman.

I was rather puzzled though when Richie suggested sheltering from a few drops of rain that were falling. We slipped unseen into an outhouse. "Eggs," explained the lad briefly. Now, I have said nothing of Richie's activities as an egg collector for he had practised it long before I met him. It was his boast that he had taken eggs in every county in Scotland and I believed him.

He got out his tea-can and disappeared into a shed from whence came the sound of hens. It was unfortunate that the farmer met him coming out! But Richie was equal to the occasion. "Aye, aye," he said. The farmer did not acknowledge but asked bluntly, "What do you want?" His tone was rude.

"I was wondering, while sheltering from the rain, whether you had any eggs to sell," said Richie easily.

The farmer eyed the can and said with some heat, "You mean you were wondering if I had any eggs for stealing. Well, you can take yourself off. There's nothing for you here."

Richie bridled. "Listen," he said, "if I had wanted eggs I could have taken them from in there. I just wanted to see if you kept any hens before disturbing you at your work."

"You knew the eggs in there were bad. That's why you didn't take them."

"How was I to know they were bad?" demanded Richie.

"Because the shells are shiny and you can smell them. Anyone knows a bad egg when they smell one."

"Listen," said Richie in a tolerant voice, "I am a plumber. If you want to know anything about pipes, brass pipes, copper pipes, bronze pipes, steel pipes, I can tell you something about them. If your taps are leaking or your pipes burst I can do something about them. That's my job. I'm not a farmer, therefore I know nothing about eggs. I asked you if you had any eggs to sell and I don't even get a civil answer. Civility costs nothing, and now that the rain is off, we'll get going. Come on, Tommy."

We left. Not without a trace of dignity either. Down the road a bit Richie laughed gleefully. Obviously we had scored a victory. I do not think he missed the eggs.

Next day saw us back home. My mother was quite shocked by my appearance. She declared I was like a greyhound, skin and bone. Certainly an examination in the mirror showed a pinched appearance and an emaciated look about the face.

But I enjoyed that trip, and even now as I write after all these years, I can still catch something of the high adventure of exploration. The Highlands were my Himalayas, and no intrepid spirit wandering new valleys in Kashmir or the Karakoram has reached a higher plane of exultation in the joy of the quest. The hardship served only to make it seem all the more worth while.

I have a lot to thank Richie for. He went to work in England shortly afterwards and our hill-partnership was severed. He was a good companion and a character. I have tried to draw him as he was, with his weakness for argument and eggs, his huge appetite, and his generosity it carrying my rucksack when I felt ill. Richie was an unconventional type of man, but no one delighted more in the wild beauty of the Highland hills, and his spirit of adventure was forever an inspiration to me.

Years later, heading for the Fannichs, I was cycling through Strathconon. It was early May and snow showers and a vicious east wind made a winter's day of it. My bike was loaded with food and camping equipment. Whisking down a hill with my load wobbling I saw a rather bald head bent over handlebars, and a pair of bare knees moving up and down in the motion of cycling endeavour against adverse circumstances. He looked up as I approached and I jammed on my brakes. It was Richie— a delightful surprise. We shook hands heartily and exchanged ideas.

He was unemployed again, and had been out of Glasgow since Friday afternoon. This was Sunday. He had left Glasgow at four o'clock in the afternoon, slept at Crianlarich, pushed through Glen Coe and up the Great Glen, through Glen Shiel and by Loch Duich to Strome Ferry on Saturday, and now he was *en route* for Fort William to spend the night there so as to be in Glasgow on Monday.

I gasped. A motorist would consider this a good tour and Richie was doing it by pushbike. He looked at my ancient bike with horror and wondered how I managed to push such a load on it. I reminded him of my early training in pack-carrying at his hands. The snowswept hills seemed very bleak after Richie passed.

3

The Cuillin

. . . I have no spur
To prick the sides of my intent, but only
Vaulting ambition, which o'er leaps itself . . .
MACBETH

THE chief joy of that celebrated library of Glasgow—the Mitchell—was, for Matt and I, the bound volumes of the *Scottish Mountaineering Club Journal*. Every Tuesday evening we used to go there, and seated at a table with three or four thick volumes, lose ourselves in following the early doings of the first club members through the Highlands.

Matt had a notebook into which went quotations, mainly descriptions of beauty, which particularly took his fancy. Into my note-book went ideas for tours suggested by what was most attractive in my available material. I am afraid I was more of a materialist, caring more for technical difficulty and inaccessibility, rather than for the natural beauty of the hills alone. Immaturity is my only excuse. In the light of my subsequent maturity I have realized that it is a phase in the lives of most climbers. Unfortunately some never pass out of it!

Soon I had, out of proportion to other districts, quite a stack of notes on Skye, extolling the ferocity of the Cuillin and the wildness of their gaunt crags. There was a description of the view from Sgùrr Alisdair too, a view over oceans and islands, sea lochs and the massed mainland hills from Torridon to Kintail and Knoydart. The rock-climbs sounded in my ears "the Crack of Doom", "the Inaccessible Pinnacle", "the Slab and Groove", "the pinnacle route of Sgùrr nan Gillean".

Matt is a prudent man and he was wary of my ambitions. Diffidently I suggested we should go to the Cuillin. He was dubious of our ability but confessed he had thought of it

See Skye map, page 67.

himself more than once. Our good friend John MacNair was sounded and was immediately enthusiastic. We had eighty feet of rope. So it was arranged for August. I bought the Scottish Mountaineering Club's *Isle of Skye* guide-book and passed the waiting months following dotted lines and reading up the climbs.

At last came the great day when the Sunday excursion train bore Matt and I to Mallaig. Matt carried a great parcel in addition to his huge rucksack bulging with climbing rope, etc. The apparent amusement of the townsfolk as we staggered through the streets looking for a camping spot mortified me, for I knew we were a strange pair, Matt with his six feet of height, and I barely five feet four inches doing my best to keep upright at the drag of an immense load of gear. There was no boat till Monday, when John would join us, hence the reason for our camping. We were too enthusiastic to wait in Glasgow till Monday.

Half a mile out of the town we struck a nice spot and camped down, snugly walled out of the wind. From a little hill one thousand feet above the tent we watched a stormy sunset over the Cuillin. For a moment the clouds parted and the magic mountains were revealed as in my fondest dream. Adventure had taken shape. The sea paled to grey as the shafts of fiery sunlight were withdrawn. The waning clouds dropped over the black bristles of Sgùrrs, and a blast of wind sent shivers through us. Quickly we ran down to the nook. It was cosy that night, listening to the beat of the sea and the steady drumming of rain on our little tent.

Morning brought John. In lashing rain at dusk we arrived in Sligachan. We eyed the place in distaste. "What a hole," said Matt, and that went for all of us. There was nothing to be seen but evil-looking peat-hags stretching to infinity, a palatial hotel, and a foaming burn. The Cuillin black and red were temporarily (we hoped) missing. We walked a bit of the glen but the sodden bogs offered no hope, so on a green spot outside the hotel, the only green spot we could find, we dropped our tent and crawled inside it.

Somehow there was room for the three of us. Matt contorted his huge frame into a bow, John made himself into a humpback, and I being little, could sit cross-legged with only my head bent to avoid our three-foot-six-high roof. We contrived a meal,

though at first the manipulation of it down the gullet was difficult. But we had a good deal of practice coming to us!

Bedding down was the next problem. We had three blankets
and I was elected centre man. Now the other two very naturally
wanted to keep themselves off the wet walls of the tent, so a
squeezing match was begun with myself as the unfortunate
buffer. We did not sleep for a long time, and when I awoke,
Matt was clawing furiously at his head. John had disappeared
below the blankets. Suddenly I was aware of a fierce irritation
attacking my face, ears, and head. The midges had arrived.
Matt produced a bottle of lotion and from the depths a hand
came up for a drop. Then one of us thrust a head out of the
midge-plagued tent. The Cuillin were clear.

What a sight that was! Even as three heads were thrust out,
a tendril of vapour made a screen revealing to us a pinnacle,
sharper and more precipitous than our dreams. We had breakfast and were away to the hill in no time. All our sorrows were
forgotten as we climbed to the foot of the first pinnacle in the
still air of that expectant morning.

From the Bhaisteir Gorge we saw two prominent chimneys on
the face of the first pinnacle and up to the foot of the right-hand
one we went. Despite the years that have elapsed since that
thrill of putting on the rope and watching Matt lead upward on
our first Cuillin climb, I can remember every detail of our route.
To us, it was a new route, chosen for its spectacular appearance,
but there were nail marks on it, and a difficult stride on an exposed place near the top. Then came the glorious scramble over
the pinnacles; the descent of the third pinnacle which, pictured
in the guide, had struck me with awe; the sound of our voices
coming back to us telling us that we were on Knight's Peak; and
the downpour of rain that met us on the misty top. We stood
on the top of Sgùrr nan Gillean like conquerors.

The main idea was to get out of the rain as quickly as possible.
Which way back? We were in rather a dilemma and were just
about to try a route when we heard voices. Here was advice
for the asking. We waited and were soon rallied by a cry for
help. The party had come up the tourist route and wanted a
rope over the summit slab which was slightly exposed. We
obliged and were told to follow the ridge and go down the first
gully. We thought we were in clover.

Soon we were bashing down a scree gully happy at the
thought of dry clothes and food which were as good as ours. A
warning shout from our leader and our mad gallop ended
abruptly. The scree from our feet was pouring over a great
crag which was a cascade of falling water. Silently we donned
the rope and pushed the descent. There was no escaping
the obstacle. The tourist route was evidently in some other
direction.

There was nothing romantic in that chilling descent, but at
last we got to the foot of the slabs of sliding water. We had no
idea where we were but just followed our way down. A length
of green glen and a huge boulder loomed ahead. "The Bloody
Stone," said Matt. We agreed before we had grasped its impli-
cations. We were in Harta Corrie on the wrong side of the
mountain: at least we knew where we were.

Through the gloom of Glen Sligachan we trudged, wet and
weary, splashing through burns and bogs. Darkness was falling
when we got to the tent. Then came the problem of changing,
for inside only one man could manipulate his clothes. So the
first man changed his clothes and came out, the second did like-
wise, and after the third had changed, the other two crawled in,
tied up the door, and we got some heat going. We slept that
night undisturbed by midges or each other.

All next day the rain peltered down. John told us a cheery
story of a cycling tour he had abandoned in similar weather for
the comforts of home. We tried to beat that one and from our
experience the Highlands had given us plenty of material. In
between times we ate and ate for want of anything better to do,
so much so that by the following morning a serious food situation had arisen. Our grand plan of girdling the Cuillin was
obviously going to be done on short commons.

Down Glen Sligachan to Loch an Athain was our next move.
Evening saw us on the top of Blaven with scudding mists revealing fragments of the depths below. The rain had gone, and despite
overcast skies we were in high spirits with the fun of climbing on
dry rock. Our camp by the shores of the little mountain-bound
loch seemed to me a very romantic place.

Packing up the following morning on a breakfast of tinned
fish and gabbro-like brown bread was not so romantic. Our
larder was empty and there was no more food to be had short of

Glen Brittle. Mournfully we breasted the rise of Druim na h-Eine and dropped down to Loch Coruisk, just a black loch, boulder strewn, making a floor for the inky clouds.

John was leading and suddenly he stopped: "I don't believe it," he said. But there they were, a bevy of ladies in gay dresses picking their dainty way along the shore. Cheery waves and cries of greeting came as they spotted us. Smiling, we drew nearer but were disconcerted to see the enthusiasm relax as we approached for inspection.

The explanation? The dear ladies had promised to deliver a parcel of food to some climbing relatives of theirs at Loch Coruisk. They had sailed over from Elgol. More important to us was the fact that they had only an hour to spare before the tide would compel them to leave.

We offered our sympathy, gave assurances that we had seen no other climbers, talked solidly of this and that for a fateful hour, and then took charge of the parcel. Our offer of money was rejected, but we were to divide the spoils if we met the rightful owners. The boat pulled out and quickly we sought a good spot for a meal.

What a parcel that was! There were eggs, bananas, jam, butter, lovely new bread, cakes, biscuits, oranges, etc. It was manna from heaven. Even the weather raised a smile to light the coast and us with warm sunshine. Replete after that banquet, we vowed Skye was the finest place we had ever been in.

Then came the part of the day that is even now a painful memory, the coastal route to Glen Brittle, a route of heart-breaking ups and downs, over boulders, screes, ambitious heather and higher bracken. We were all feeling the weight of our ruck-sacks. My neck was stiff with the hours of carrying, and we seemed to be walking endlessly. About a mile from the glen, on the dried-up bed of an old water-course we pitched our tent. The only flat spot was right on the edge of a sea cliff but we were much too tired to care.

Later the moon rose, sending a lane of silver across the water. From the gabbro sands came sounds I grew to love, the shrill pipings of mingled oyster-catchers and redshank. At our backs, wedged against the dark sky, were the peaks, sliced cleaner and sharper than any we had ever seen before.

Adventure is a comparative thing. To us, youngsters in experience, tackling the most difficult peaks in Scotland was savouring at its highest the joys of the unknown. We did not know
whether our skill would be equal to the task and that is the
essence of all adventure. It was this feeling of uncertainty that
made us tingle with anticipation as we clambered to the foot of
that great buttress of Sgùrr Alasdair on which we knew was
a route called Collie's Climb.

The great crag disappeared into mist. Coire Lagain and that
terrific precipice of Sròn na Cìche overwhelmed us with perpendicularity. It was with difficulty that I persuaded Matt to
attempt a number three climb, that being the classification of
Collie's Climb—which means difficult. At eighteen I felt that
for his twenty-two years Matt was over-cautious. He was capable of leading anything, I felt certain, and only needed a bit of
coaxing. Such was my belief, nor have I had cause to alter it
over the years. Had it been otherwise I am afraid I would have
sent Matt to his death before this, for the stupidity of my youthful ambitions was extreme. John was willing to go anywhere—
the ideal companion.

We put on the rope and the ascent sped. The climb was
"steep and spectacular", as the book had said. Mist swirled
round us and the rocks were dripping wet when we came to the
bad bit. John and I were in a little cave. I remember a spike
of rock but we had no idea how to use it as a belay. Matt
crept outward on to the perpendicular wall with the whole
length of the climb below him. He came back to us looking
worried. "Well, if that's rock-climbing, I'm no rock-climber,"
he said. His tone was grim. "Take a look at it," he said to me.

I had a look and was in the act of stepping up to do battle
with it when he called me back. John wanted to have a try but
Matt said "Just a minute". He went out and up in his effortless
and bold style. That is ever Matt's way. If there is a risk to
take, he is the man to take it. Steep rock on good holds and we
were on the tiny summit of the Cuillin's highest point, exultant.

Then came the traverse of Sgùrr Theàrlaich, a fine climb on
Sgùrr Mhic Coinnich, glimpses of the wild peak of An Stac and
a glorious scramble over it to the Inaccessible Pinnacle, up by
the short side and down the long. How happily we came down
the An Stac screes that night! We had done the round of Coire

Lagain—a mountaineer's day. The achievement was a stepping-stone to bigger things.

Long before we were off the Cuillin we noticed lightning flashing far out at sea, but took no particular heed of it. Back at camp we had a meal, got the beds down, and, weary after our hard day's climb, were soon asleep.

About half-past one in the morning we were awakened by a terrific clap of thunder. The rain came down as though turned on by a tap; rain that came through the tent as though the canvas did not exist. In a few moments our water-course was no longer dried up, but a foaming burn that washed over our blankets and gear. Lightning lit up the tent for seconds at a time and the thunder was a continuous roar; a roar, half of which was echo, for the Cuillin threw back every peal, ripping and crackling across the sky.

For an hour and a half the storm continued unabated and I had visions of being washed over that sea cliff which was our front door. In the first lull we packed up and forced a route to Glen Brittle. I say forced, because every burn was an obstacle and I fell into most of them, once up to my neck, and would have been under had not Matt's strong arm supported me. Each of us in turn got a ducking.

There was a newly opened schoolhouse as Youth Hostel in those days, and after invading the ladies' quarters—a mistake which yielded a few blankets as well as shrieks of alarm—we got down to it on the common-room floor for a few hours; but sleep was out of the question.

Bitter for John, the morning dawned fine and he had to leave us for the walk to Sligachan and home. With a wave, he slung his sodden blanket into the sea and declared he had had a great time. "I'll be back next year too," he vowed.

We thought of him as we crossed from Sgùrr Dearg to Sgùrr a' Mhadaidh—that glorious day of shifting mist which gave us our finest "Brocken Spectre", a beautiful circle of rainbow with our great shadows flickering puppet-like in the centre. We each had one, and for several minutes they remained with us. There were dramatic moments too, with the black ridges smoking vapour and openings in the clouds revealing wedges and shapes where we thought the sun should be. It was moonlight when we came down An Tàirneilear and I found myself thinking more of the beauty of the Cuillin and the wonder of their views than the technical difficulty of the rocks.

Our high hopes of a good day to follow were hopes indeed. Of the Cuillin there was nothing to be seen except the bog that rises behind Glen Brittle House. It is a long, long day in Glen Brittle if you do not climb, so after watching the creeping mists and smirr of rain falling for a while we decided to go on to the tops and chance it. In five hours we were soaked to the skin and as miserable with cold as any two humans could be. Crossing from Sgumain to Alasdair in a wind of gale force with slashing rain that struck with the solidity of beads remains a vivid memory. I felt slightly ashamed at asking for the rope on the bad step between the two peaks, but I know now that that little bit of prudence was worth a lot of pride.

The next day was an epic one for me. We climbed the Cioch. By much coaxing I got Matt to try his hand on the direct route, but after two hundred feet he jibbed at the bulge. I wanted to try it but was called back after ten feet or so. Matt was taking no chances. However, we traversed on to the west route and were enthralled by its vast exposure and exciting finish on the steepest mountain wall that I know. Most of the way it rained, and by the time we came down the eastern gully we were well soaked again. I was beginning to feel rather proud of myself now and no mean climber.

"The Slab and Groove" was a name I liked the sound of. Imagine the thrill of coming back to the hostel and answering nonchalantly to the question of what did you do: "Oh, we did the Slab and Groove—Mallory's climb, you know."

Now, among the other campers washed out by the storm were a bunch of Manchester climbers, the star performer of which was one, Harry Pearson, a man who had made a name for himself in the Lakes and on the gritstone crags of Derbyshire. An accident to his foot had prevented his climbing for days past, but now he was going up the Cioch and nothing less than the Slab and Groove would satisfy him. The day was wet and windy and one by one the climbers in the hostel turned down the proposition. Matt was emphatically not for it. "Above my standard," he said. But I with stupidity and ignorance of extreme youth was agog with enthusiasm. We set off, I with one hundred feet of rope over my shoulder, feeling like Alexander Burgener.

Under the low mists the black rocks dripped dismally. Wind smote against the face with explosive sounds. "A mug's game in this weather," said Harry as he undid the rope beneath what appeared to be an unclimbable overhang. "Yes, it goes up there all right," said Harry. "So this is what a super-severe rock climb looks like," I thought. It took a lot of care that first pitch. The second pitch led us to "the Slab", which Mallory, the climber who pioneered it and who was later killed on Mount Everest, did not think would "go" in wet conditions.

There was a good belay and I watched Harry's tricouni nails edge their way upward and across that smooth bit of rock sensationally set between two overhangs. Below there was a clean drop to the screes. Water was cascading over the protruding lip of the other one on to our slab. I could see Harry was finding it hard going. He was perhaps twenty feet from me and twenty feet up when he stuck (I quote that from a twelve-year-old memory).

For a long time he maintained a straddled position, legs far apart, then suddenly he reached downward, grasped a small thumb of rock and hung out on it. Hanging on with one hand he rubbed furiously at his leg with the other. "Cramp!" he shouted. "Unrope quick, I'm going to abseil." Quickly he took in the rope, hand over hand, over his small handhold till both ends were about equal in length. He then looped it round the thumb and grasping both ends below it, he hung outwards, passing the rope under his legs and over his shoulder. Seated thus in his loop of rope he rested, for it must have been desperate work taking that rope in, supported by only one hand. I had no idea what he was doing. All I knew was that he was in a perilous position and it was impossible for me to give him any help.

Then I saw his strategy. He relaxed his hold on the rope and his weight on the loop caused a sort of pulley motion. So, using his legs to keep him from spinning on the steep face, he reached a position slightly below me. The problem was to get on to my stance. Pushing himself with jabs of his right leg his body swung like a pendulum, wider and wider till one great arc brought him within reach of my clutching hand. "Did you think I was done for?" he said. A tiny flick and the rope came away from the little thumb that had saved his life. I had my introduction to the exciting art of abseiling coming down the two hundred feet or so which we had climbed. I do not know whether Harry was joking or not when he said he owed not a little of his skill to constant practice from his bedroom window.

Sunlight, real sunlight, flooded the glen as Matt and I packed up the following morning. This was our last climbing day, and as we had to go to Sligachan, we decided to carry our gear to the top of the Bealach a' Mhàim and do a climb on the north side of the range. Matt was all for reaching the tops quickly to enjoy the view but I persuaded him to try the north chimney on Bruach na Frìthe saying it was only "difficult" and would probably not take so very long. I nearly sent Matt to his death that day.

At one point high up on this climb, an overhanging chock-stone is encountered which according to the "guide" is overcome by threading the rope through a hole in the cave, swinging out on to the face, and proceeding thereafter up the wall. Matt was all against the idea. With my usual presumption I wanted to get swinging but Matt was firm. He was all for turning back but I pointed out how easily Collie's Climb had "gone" to a determined attack, and probably this would be the same.

My "sales talk" won and Matt swung out of sight with a great scraping of nails. The minutes passed and the rope went up very slowly. Small sounds of scraping and heavy breathing just reached me. After what seemed an age there was a shout. I could not make out what he was saying but I shouted back and was heaved into the air on to the face. My hands explored for holds and my feet scraped and scratched but I just could not find anything at all. Inch by inch Matt pulled me up, and not for fifteen feet or so could I find anything on this holdless wall. "That's the worst place I've ever been in," said Matt emphatically. "I was on the edge of coming off the whole way up." I felt rather ashamed of myself but Matt, always tactful, eased my feelings by adding: "Still, it was a good thing." I do not disagree with J. B. Wright's classification of this climb as a severe one.

Not a breath of wind stirred as we reached that glorious view-point of the Bruach. Over the sea to the Isles was ours: the full beauty of the Cuillin which we were seeing for the first time was startling. These were the tops we had climbed, all clear at last. To the north-east were the Torridon hills over which John and I had wandered a year before.

It was a vasty panorama. But there was an axe-tooth of rock beckoning, destroying our peace of mind till it was climbed, the Bhaisteir Tooth. We chose Naismith's route and exulted in its beautiful finish, steep and exposed on small but good holds. From Am Bhaisteir, the glory of the west as the sunset was worth every drop of rain that contributed to the painted landscape. I cannot describe the incredible colours of the Cuillin, or the subtle tints of the changing sea.

Dusk was well on the way to night when we arrived at Sligachan. The midges had lost none of their ferocity but after such a day nothing could dampen our soaring spirits.

"A great holiday," said Matt. That summed it up!

4

The Autumn Cuillin

W<small>HEN</small> you have lost count of the number of times you have been to a place, it can be said, I think, that you know that place pretty well. That is my position with the Cuillin. It would be laborious if I recounted every trip my diaries tell me that I made to these wonderful mountains between 1933 and the time of writing in 1946. But of all those trips, two are outstanding; the sun shone, and for a time I was no longer a soldier.

For company I had an A.T.S. girl, my friend Matt's niece, Margaret Campbell, who wanted very much to see Skye. The month was September and as we circled round the heather purple hills to Achnashellach, all the tops were clear and every lochan reflected the grey rocks, rust of bracken, and variety of hill form. To Margaret it was a new world of beauty, and her delight in it all made explanation superfluous.

Past Fuar Tholl and Sgorr Ruadh we rolled down to Strath Carron and on the Kyle of Lochalsh. What a journey that was! The sea was calm, greeny-blue and sprinkled at the edge with weed that was yellow gold. Looking back along the line and across Loch Carron the eye ranged the grey peaks of Torridon down to the bulky tops of Applecross. To the west was Skye, signposted by the shapely spire of Sgùrr nan Gillean and the South Cuillin soaring over the Red Hills. Slanting sunrays made a beautiful foreground, picking out the intervening ridges with golden light.

Soon we were on the ferry and skirting by bus the sea coast to Sligachan. In the little fields beside the crofts the old people and the very young were busy at the corn. Pitiful little fields of short weedy corn, but the peat smoke scenting the air and the romantic setting of mountain and sea, I felt, were compensation enough for the most primitive of crops. On long wooden racks hay was spread to dry. I thought of Kent, where the tall corn was long gathered and a second crop of hay had been taken.

Then came glimpses of shattered rock, Clach Glas and Blaven

peeping over the shoulder of a red peak. A sweep round a bend and there they were, the Black Cuillin, with Sgùrr nan Gillean, Am Bhaisteir, the Tooth, gigantic, towering above the glowing moor. How vivid Glen Sligachan was, with the contrasting tones of the Black Cuillin on one side, and on the other side the glistening screes and fierce tints of the truly Red Hills. Raasay, the heather island, was at the height of its blooming, a marvel of tone quality floating on blue seas. Never have I seen such a feast of colour.

We put our kit in the hotel and strolled up the Mam. The sunlight had retreated towards the tops leaving the glen in shadow. Away to the north, the Storr was a beautiful shade lit by soft light. Near at hand, was the crag of Clach Glas and the mighty blue shadow which was the vastness of Blaven. We had the pinnacles in profile when the moon rose over the silhouetted blade of the third. Soon it was a silvery three-quarters as the gloaming deepened. We did not say much, Margaret and I. It was that kind of night.

Indoors it was cheery in Sligachan, for an old climbing acquaintance and a friend had just come down from the pinnacles, so we had much to say to each other.

By a great piece of luck we were able to arrange for our bags to be delivered to Glen Brittle. I interrogated Margaret as to what she wanted to do, explaining the alternatives: an easy crossing by the Bealach a' Mhàim or a hard walk down Glen Sligachan and across the Cuillin to Glen Brittle. My bias was, of course, obvious, and we set off down the glen.

It was a morning in a thousand, crisp air, brilliant skies, and the sun gaining strength. The colours were even more vivid than on the preceding evening. Margaret has a lovely voice and we sang Gaelic songs as we walked. The south peaks against the blue of that sky was a sight to remember. Above us in Harta Coire the grey screes and slabs of bending rock were marvellously inviting.

Over the ridge of Druim nan Ràmh we climbed and from the top had Loch Coruisk and its wonderful setting below us. Every shade of blue was there, varying in tint from dark to where the mainland hills made a fairy picture of light beyond Loch Scàvaig. Poor Margaret felt the climb hard but stuck it manfully and faced the thousand feet of rocky descent with equanimity.

Across the great hollow of Coruisk the serrated shadows of the towering peaks were thrown in shimmering mauve.

A bite of food at the loch-side and we started up the Bealach Coire na Banachdaich. It was a weary slipping on screes but at last we topped the ridge and below us was Loch Brittle and beyond, the Outer Isles. "Two or three hundred feet more and you can say you have climbed one of the Cuillin," I coaxed, but Margaret was satisfied where she was. She selected a little sun trap while I ran off over Sgùrr na Banachdaich and Thormaid.

The Cuillins gave me their best that evening. The Coire Lagain peaks with the sun on the long back of Sgù Mhic Coinnich; the Dubhs, ebony black, the colour of their name; Blaven a glory of dappled blue; ". . . the great brown slabs bending over into immeasurable space", at my feet; the face of Ghreadaidh wrinkled with shadows and bristling bright where the sun touched; Portree in the bay and beyond, the Storr; silvery tints on the sea and the Outer Islands like clean clouds on the horizon; the intense blueness of Rùm and Canna; all were a reward worth waiting a lifetime for.

Margaret was asleep when I got back but uncomplainingly stirred herself for the descent. All the corrie was flooded rose-red as we made our leisurely way downward. Only Margaret's indomitable spirit kept her going, but she made it. At the house we got the usual fine welcome, and with a good meal inside us and the fire blazing we had a grand *céilidh*. I felt I had come home.

Nancy, the terror of Glen Brittle House, but the climber's friend, woke me early for I wanted to climb as well as see that Margaret was kept amused. Up Coire Lagain under the dark vastness of perpendicularity which is Sròn na Cìche I went. The north-west buttress of Sgùrr Sgumain saw me to the top and, as always, I was captivated by the beautiful points of Ghreadaidh and Mhadaidh opposite. A light rain fell as I traversed Alasdair and soon a gusty wind was blowing. Over Theàrlaich, a sporting route on Mhic Coinnich, An Stac and the Inaccessible Pinnacle, and I enjoyed it immensely. We finished up, Margaret and I, by assisting at the harvest that evening.

Next day was uneventful except for a climb on the window buttress and a walk to the Rhu to count some cattle. The day was heavy and still, with occasional sunshine. The effects on the

South Cuillin were fine indeed. Now and again their sombre grey-blue would light up and cloud-shadows sprinkle themselves on the slopes. Over the wee loch on the point were the cattle, hidden in various hollows but at last we had them counted. By the green grass of an old ruin were a pair of wheatears. Thrushes and blackbirds were there too, and I glimpsed a wren and a dunnock, so the birds had not forsaken the old habitation. We had a merry time with the harvesters that night.

Margaret's leave had now expired so I saw her over to Sligachan. She was for the south of England, and I was for an attempt on the Cuillin ridge—all of it.

The sun was shining and there was a great stillness over everything, a stillness emphasized by a haze which gave height and distance to the peaks. Peculiarly wild and formidable they looked. I had been looking forward to a view from the top of Sgùrr nan Gillean, but with my usual luck on this peak a mist formed while I was on the pinnacles and that was how it was on top.

Getting on to Am Bhaisteir was easy enough but getting off it to the "Tooth" not so easy. Now the rain set in good and proper and a real blanket descended. All went well if wetly till the centre peak of Bidenn Druim nan Ràmh when I found myself on very steeply dropping rock unscratched by nailmarks. Obviously there was something wrong. I climbed back upward and waited for a clearing but without much hope.

But luck was with me. A brightness opening to a mighty shadow which was a peak came after ten minutes. Climbing quickly I gained the top and for a moment the boiling mists swirled above the Cuillin. It was a spectacular vision of immensity and savage mountainland. I saw my ridge and was soon tackling its peculiar little difficulties, one of which was quite awkward. Over the four tops of Sgùrr a' Mhadaidh I scrambled and at the An Dorus gap headed for home. I was soaking wet and there was nothing to be seen, so I felt I was doing the wisest thing. A bath and a Glen Brittle house-dinner, the good society of the MacRaes, and I was as happy as a king.

I did not object to the misty day of rain that followed for I felt like a spell indoors to enjoy a book and the comforts of home. It cleared in the evening, however, so I had a walk. From the shore I could see the clouds were heaving in Coire Lagain, revealing ribs of rock edging upward into space, pinnacles detached and enormous flitting behind veils of grey, squares and curves of black floating in the sky; magic glimpses indeed. It was nearly as good as being on the tops.

Over the bay ringed plover were flying in small flocks, gannets wheeled and dived, and inshore cormorants and mergansers were fishing. I visited the old "black house" on the hill behind the post office. What a filth of darkness and insanitation it was: it was difficult to believe that only eight months before this place had been lived in.

Brother and sister lived in it. Their beds were side by side and sunk in the wall. Rotting wood laid unevenly and sparsely over the bare earth which was the floor. One tiny window, with a few sprigs of dying bog myrtle in pots decorating it, admitted light. Inside, there were two chambers, one of which boasted a fireplace against the wall. The thatch leaked and the place smelt abominably. No wonder old Dr. Johnson had a lot of things to say against the Highlands!

Of course, all "black houses" are not as in the condition described, but this is an example of the very primitive ones with no suggestion of the improvements which most "black house" dwellers have incorporated over the years. That night Captain Ramsay of the Scottish Horse turned up.

Over breakfast we discussed what we would climb. The Captain was for the "Slab and Groove", but the conditions of wind and rain were even worse than on my previous attempt on this climb. Had I known the Captain's ability I would not have put him off without at least trying it.

We got to the foot of the rocks and explored around like a couple of lost spirits. "Let's start up the Median route anyway," said Ramsay. At first we led alternate pitches, but the high wind threatening to brush us from the crags quite disconcerted me, and at the fan-shaped trap pitch I handed over the lead to the better man.

Despite the appalling conditions the Captain wanted more difficulty, so we traversed left to a groove and an overhang of some severity. Above it, slabs led to another groove and an overhang. This latter was a tough nut to crack. Ramsay, being a six-footer, was able to get a leg on to some trap on the left. I had to cling a way up and I think it was severe enough to satisfy

the exacting requirements of the man himself. As I had no belay
and the exposure was all the way up, it certainly satisfied me.

On top there was no escaping the murderous wind, and it was
hard work going over Sgumain and Alasdair. Even the Captain
did not fancy the bad step that day. The face of Sgùrr Theàrlaich was just a sliding waterfall of rain which, every time a gust
of wind hit it, cascaded in a spout over us. I was relieved when
the suggestion was put forward that we should descend rather
than "do" the Dubhs. It was a joy afterwards to change out of
our wet things, have a bath and dinner, and chat comfortably by
the fireside.

Next day I had to leave. The Cuillin were in mist but on the
coast by Broadford the sun was shining brightly on the purple
moors. At Armadale I had a shock. The boat, owing to the
previous day's storm, had not yet left the Outer Isles, so there
was nothing for it but to hang around. I went to the local inn.

In the bar was an old toothless man who regarded me steadily
with glassy eyes. His drooping moustache and fresh complexion
had an alcoholic look. I ordered him a double whisky and a
half pint of beer. That began a long story in Gaelic. Now and
again he burst into a singing wail. Luckily an interpreter was
at hand or the performance would have been lost to me. The
tale was of a potato famine and how one man had plenty of
potatoes and the other had none. The man with none was
something of a bard, so he composed a song to the man with
plenty. This wail, extolling the virtues of the potato-plenty
man was the song. It resulted in a pooling of potato resources.

At last, as a wild sunset flamed over Canna and Rùm the
boat drew into Mallaig. A fish train was commissioned into
service and twenty-four hours later I arrived in Dover, worn out
with travel, but not regretting a thing.

5

The Winter Cuillin

Four a.m. is the wrong time to hold a debate on any station platform, least of all one as cold and windswept as Aviemore Junction on a January morning. Arthur Pearson and I had arranged to climb in the Cairngorms, an arrangement which did not take into account two feet of new snow and more falling. This meant that the peaks would not be in condition for days. In the short debating time at our disposal, I extolled the mildness of the western seaboard in comparison to this central area and, plumbing my experience in support of suitable propaganda, produced such a weight of evidence, that Arthur jumped aboard the train confidently expecting me to take him to snow in just the correct proportions for mountaineering. By the time we got to Inverness I had talked him into going to Skye.

It is a sorrowful business arriving at Inverness bleary-eyed from want of sleep, and at a time when no connections to the north are available. The only place was the lounge of the Station Hotel and we lay there from six a.m. till the porter stirred us with a reminder that we were not guests.

Our connecting train was woefully late, owing to the snow, and in the morning sunshine we bemoaned our decision about Skye as we tramped the streets of Inverness. But the die was cast.

At last, when we had almost given up hope of ever getting away, our train pulled in and we were off. The afternoon light was at its best as we edged round the Beauly Firth and sped towards the dazzling bulk of Ben Wyvis. Little parties of duck and divers were in the bays, casting their reflections in the vivid-blue water of the placid firth. Some Bewick's swans came as a surprise and were close enough inshore to make identification easy.

But my prediction as to the mildness of the west was steadily being given the lie, for the farther west we went the deeper became the snow. But around us was a fairy scene, for each tree and shrub was in blossom with frost crystals, and pine bark was

31

red and shining. Loch Carron was a mirror for the afterglow
on its snowy mountains, and as always, the Torridon mountains
seemed enormous.

In the grey light of dusk we threaded the cold landscape and
black lochs to Sligachan, the chains rattling on the bus-tyres as
they crunched frozen snow. A telephone call, and a car was
forthcoming to take us to Glen Brittle. Swinging, sliding, and
jolting we got over the frozen track to the house of the kindly
MacRaes. As always, homecoming to me.

Getting out of bed into the darkness and cold of the morning
took a bit of will power. The Cuillin were grey touched with
fire as we climbed. As yet, the Outer Isles were dark in a dull
sea but clear cut and sharp. Below us, every wrinkle in the moor
was picked out, with shadows making folds of the deep snow.
Arthur's game leg, the result of an air crash, was giving him
trouble, so at a thousand feet when the tops were floodlit yellow
in a deep blue sky, he had to give up.

I went on and clambered up Sgùrr Dearg. It was hard going,
for the choice was between sinking into deep snow or taking to
ice-covered rocks. Higher up, there was no choice and it was
great fun tackling an infinite variety of forms; verglas; sheet ice;
ice crystals; and even pure névé. Not a scrap of the original
rock was showing on Dearg except for the south face of the
Inaccessible Pinnacle. But, as ice crowned the exits of the possible routes on that face, I think the pinnacle was really inaccessible. From every other standpoint it was just a glistening finger
of ice.

Views from the summit were impressive. Sròn na Cìche,
banded with ice, looked absolutely impregnable; and the great
faces of Alasdair, Theàrlaich, and Mhic Coinnich the last word
in inaccessibility. Blaven and Clach Glas bristled with hanging
snow and ice, but it was my immediate peaks that attracted most
since I was going to try my hand on them.

It was interesting work. The ordinary scree slopes on top
were converted into sheets of steep ice-crystals consolidated like
névé, which meant that at any angle at all, steps had to be cut.
All the rocks had a moss if ice-flowers, very easily cleared, but
sometimes it was underlaid with glazed stuff. Snow texture was
varied too and took a little practice before the eye could assess
its behaviour. Progress was reasonably fast, however, and after

Banachdaich I felt I had its measure and technique. Thormaid was difficult, and I nearly gave up on Ghreadaidh but fortunately a justifiable route presented itself and I was able to get across to Mhadaidh. That windless frosty day of sunshine was the finest, I think, I have ever spent.

Views were marvellous from here. Loch Coruisk, deep down in shadow, held the amethyst of the sunclouds. From it rose the ice-girders that supported the fluted tops. The silence was deathly. Frost gripped the water-chains that make a soundbox of Coire an Uaigneis, a soundbox of roaring water, water that slides two thousand feet from the Cuillins' heights to cascade into Loch Coruisk. There was a new atmosphere in the Cuillin which at first was beyond me to define. I thought it was this strange silence, the feeling of something missing.

Then it came to me that it was something different from the silence of the great rock basins. Atmosphere is a difficult thing to define. Atmosphere: that peculiar quality of mystery that surrounds the Cuillin, a mystery that I know now to be made up of colour—combinations of colours that change with every turn of the light. The snow and ice had taken away their individuality by clothing them in ordinary mountain garments of however fantastic design. Technically there was a gain, but to a lover of the Cuillin there was a loss.

Think of Blaven and Clach Glas robed in purple, and the edges of dark rock rising from Coruisk to the shapely peaks of the South Cuillin. Every minute the tops are changing, from purple to blue, black to grey; and if the mist is smoking in the gullies or curling over the crests the mystery is something almost tangible.

The Cuillin had been stripped of their mystery. That was it! Sunshine and snow had made of them dazzling peaks, brazen instead of shy and retiring. There was no contrasting Red Cuillin or delicately tinted Quiraing in the distance. All Scotland was mantled alike and Skye was no different. It is the complaint of Scottish climbers who go to the Alps that they miss the rich colours of home. That was what was missing in Skye.

But I had no complaints. The observation was interesting. Beyond the sea were the mainland mountains, chain on chain of peaks cut with shadows that cleft their bloodstained snows. The Long Island had crept nearer, its peaks humpbacks of darkness riding dim seas. Only a gleam on their very tops indicated snow on them, a trick of light, for I knew them to be snow-covered. Over all Skye, from the Storr Rocks to McLeod's Maidens, glowed the flush of a scarlet sun. I watched it grow in intensity, until the snows at my feet were dyed crimson, not pink, but a red I would never have believed in a painting. The whole Cuillin were on fire and the granules of snow showed their wonderous texture as though they were precious stones.

Exalted by what I had seen, I retraced my steps to the An Dorus gap and then in a glorious swoop, glissaded a full thousand feet. It was dark when I got to the house.

Now there was a captain in the Paratroops and a young cousin of his staying at the house, so we had a merry evening exchanging ideas, etc. Arthur had managed the top of Sgùrr Dearg after all, and it was good to hear his first impressions of the Alpine Cuillin. Everything was as a perfect evening should be, when in came Nancy bearing a telegram. It was for me, a peremptory message telling me to return at once to the unit.

The Captain read it. "The roads are blocked," he said, "I can verify that." We were in the act of working it all out when Nancy laughed. It was a joke. Mary Chisholm from the post office and Nancy had worked it out between them. The evening was all the better for it.

There was a bit of cloud hanging on the hills on the following morning and we talked of an impending change. But we were mistaken. Sunrise touched the tops with rose and overspread the glen in waves of yellow light. Out at sea it was beautiful, a colourful marbled pattern being formed by cloud-catching currents, or so I presumed these twistings to be. Five hundred feet above the house, by the steep side of the gorge I was astonished to hear a familiar "churr, churr" and to see a pair of long-tailed tits picking at the icy bark of a stunted birch. I would have been surprised to see them in summer, for this is not the terrain one associates with the sprite of the woodlands. Perhaps they were the very rare northern form, but I had no glass with me to make sure.

It was hard going to Coire Lagain in deep snow and I was thankful to get on to the north buttress of Sgùrr Sgumain, even if it meant climbing on iced rocks. It was a great moment when

I stepped on to the top, out of the cold into sunshine that was really warm.

From the icy spears of Ghreadaidh and Mhadaidh to the long snowy ridges of the Outer Isles was mine. Over Soay the Minch was as blue as the sky. The ridge to Alasdair was a wonderful sight, dazzling to the eye in piled snow and ice. Getting to the top was not easy, particularly as the heat of the sun was loosening boulders and huge plates of ice.

However, seated on the top and comfortably warm, with Coire Lagain on one side and Coire Ghrunnda on the other, who could have asked for more? Sitting by myself on top of the Cuillin, it was easy to traverse geological time and imagine the snowy slopes at my feet extend to the hollow of Coire Lagain, and drop from the lochan in an icefall to a great glacier that pushed its snout into the sea. What a history; of bubbling lavas consolidated into mountains of rock, then carved by water and frosts into their present forms; and the eroded corries filled with moving ice that scored and polished the rocks *en route* to the sea. Hard to believe that the slow process of time could wear away the weaker lavas till all that was left was the skeleton gabbro, gnarled and tough, with only a few ribs of basalts to tell of what had once been skin as well as frame.

Sgùrr Theàrlaich came next and gave unexpectedly a climb on dry rock free from ice or snow. My hopes of traversing Mhic Coinnich were dashed by the sight of the next portion of the ridge. It would have taken a solid day of cutting, for its steep face was armoured in shining ice that told its own tale. For compensation there was the swoop down what is normally the "stone shoot" in an exciting glissade to the lochan.

Nature was still bent on surprising me. At fourteen hundred feet in a trickle of water below Sròn na Cìche I put up a jack-snipe, and just below that place, a woodcock rose from underfoot.

That night we were joined by a Polish climber, a stranger to the Cuillin, who had done most of his climbing in the High Tatra. I was keen to try something more exciting than what I had been doing, so I suggested we should join forces and storm one of the standard climbs. Henrik was agreeable and next morning saw us plodding up Coire Banachdaich. The day was flawless and Henrik was exultant.

Frost had bound the snow and crunched underfoot. Soon we

were under the window buttress and donning the rope. Every hold had to be cleared which meant that the ice-axe was never out of the gloved hand. I should have realized from the start that the climb was too difficult for Henrik and abandoned it forthwith. Instead of that I encouraged him. I was frozen and impatient when he finally joined me on top of the first pitch.

The standard of climbing was high throughout, but it was the steep section above the pinnacle that gave most trouble. Verglas underlaid a thicker layer of plastered ice that covered every hold. It was delicate work calling for great care. Henrik was not at all happy and took an interminable time. It was late when at last we stepped on to the ridge.

Often I have been accused of being an inconsiderate fellow on mountains, but my motives were purely altruistic when I suggested that rather than return as Henrik wished, he should at least go on to the top and get the reward of the view, having come so far. Now Arthur, who is not a rock-climber, had reached the top of Dearg safely, so I had no compunction in leaving Henrik of the High Tatra to make his own way to the top while I went on, for there was the promise of an outstanding sunset.

I was seated happily at the cairn admiring the beauty of everything when from below I heard a faint wail. There was an unmistakable note of distress in it and I dashed downwards. Six hundred feet down I found Henrik, stuck in an easy place but minus his ice-axe. He had thrown it down before him at a spot where it was most important as a wedge. Luckily it had not gone more than eighty feet down an icy gully, so with the help of a doubled rope I retrieved it. Henrik still wanted to go back but I had no intention of letting him out of my sight, so we went to the top together. He sat on Dearg while I climbed An Stac.

That was a sunset in a lifetime. The whole west was a flood of colour spreading over the ocean in waves of fire and lemon and blue-green. Around me the snows were blood-coloured. But it was the mainland that fascinated me. All the tops were clear cut, from Torridon to the Mamores, and bathed in the same blood light. Never have I seen such visibility or such truly Alpine form. The whole Kyle of Lochalsh, reaching in to Loch Hourn and Loch Nevis, was molten as tinged from a furnace. After all else had paled, Ben Nevis was an arc of fire.

I joined Henrik at the foot of the Inaccessible Pinnacle and pointed out the glissade. He said he could do it all right but was keen to see me go first, so I shot away for a thousand feet until I was stopped by an ice wall nearly vertical in places, with below that, a fair drop over rock. Luckily there was a good knob for double roping and I knew we could probably traverse off, once down the ice.

To warn Henrik, I started climbing upward, but of him there was no sign. He was well up, having in fact reached his present position by climbing slowly downward, not glissading. We had no hope of getting off the mountain at that speed, for already darkness was well on the way and the stars were out. I explained as patiently as I could our position but could not persuade him to glissade.

At last we got to the knob of rock for double roping. I showed him the technique and explained its absolute safety. He was horrified at the very idea and begged me to go first to illustrate it. I got a good stance forty feet down and awaited him with words of encouragement that turned to exasperation as he hesitated and hesitated. I straddled the gully ready to catch a body as he at last started off with many cries for help, but to his astonishment, he joined me safe and sound.

An anxious ten minutes followed, but I discovered a route across a ledge and down a chimney. Henrik was now so badly shaken, I had to put his feet in the holds for him. A beautiful green light was on Alasdair and Sgumain as we touched down in Coire Lagain.

There was still a steep slope down to the lochan to be descended, so putting Henrik's legs over mine we descended in tandem, tobogganing at fair speed on our backs. I could hardly believe my ears when I heard a thin tremor of sound becoming a happy whoop for joy at the rush of speed. Henrik was enjoying his glissade. So much so, that all the way down to Glen Brittle he persisted in sliding down anything that looked like a slope. It was eight p.m. when we got in, and a great relief to every one to see us in one piece.

Now I have told this tale not for the elevation of self by illustrating my ability at another's expense, but to show how foolish it is to assume anything with chance acquaintances. Henrik's day was spoiled, for he was unhappy most of the time; my temper was on edge at his slowness in climbing and lack of technique; but above all, we were an unsafe party. I would have been safer, even on that standard of difficulty, by myself. And the same applies to Henrik. He would have been safer had he set out by himself and tackled what he felt capable of. As the late A. F. Mummery pointed out years ago, the mere addition of a man does not necessarily strengthen the party. This does not mean, of course, that it is wise to climb "severes" by oneself.

That sunset was much too vivid and I was not surprised to find grey mist and a heavy smirr of rain over everything next morning. There was unmistakably a thaw on. Once again the roaring sound of falling water filled the glen.

The Captain was going to the Storr if the roads would allow, so by his kind invitation Arthur and I joined him. And it was a bumpy journey. We got to the place in time to see the mist breaking round its great crags, each revealing trick of vapour being reflected in the ice-mirror of loch fronting it. Seeing the fantastic pinnacles grow out of the clouds that still morning was a weird other-world sight. It was nice to see patches of green grass again too.

We climbed up to the "Old Man" to see at close hand why it had never been scaled. I proposed a route, probably because I knew in the existing conditions I would not be called upon to put it to the test. It will be a bold and enterprising climber who trusts his life to those volcanic rocks at the dizzy angle of the Storr. Set on such a slender foundation and pointing its finger "agin the laws o' nature", one wonders how such a pinnacle has stood through the ages. A pair of ravens barking excitedly was appropriate sound in the wild setting. We scrambled around, saw a hen merlin dash out over the heather, and four wild swans fly out to sea.

Descended from the Storr and we headed out to the sea cliffs of the "Kilt Rock", in rain, past roaring torrents and ice-hung crags that reminded the Captain of the Rockies. All that remained now was to traverse across the hill to the other coast and come back to the house by Uig and the west. There was nothing to be seen but mile after mile of snow-scarred peat-hags inexpressibly dreary in the grey drizzle.

For the next two days it rained. The mist was down to five hundred feet, so in lieu of climbing we went bird-watching.

Sitting above the gorge watching the milky water curving down
in a hundred foot drop to land in smoky spray out of sight was
another diversion and an inspiring one. In the evenings we
talked economics with our Polish friend but he was too much
for us and soon had us out of our depth.

The last day was a cheerless one with the sea a lifeless grey
surf. At its edge were bedraggled looking rock pipits, hoodie
crows, oyster-catchers, turnstones, clamouring gulls, and even
a pair of ravens and a buzzard. In heavy showers we crossed to
the remote point of Rhu Dunan, enjoying the sea cliffs and sitting
in a cove to watch the surf break in smothering foam. In this
little isolated hollow sheltered from the wind by its steep depth,
a blackbird came out to have a look at us and the news spread
quickly. We were objects of curiosity for no less than a hedge-
sparrow, a wren, a stonechat looking very smart in black cap and
white collar, a rock pipit, and a hermit robin. Curious how a
little place like that was so full of life when most of the coast
was empty. Probably they never left the spot or had any need
to, for all the species mentioned are sedentary, as far as birds can
be said to be so, and there was an availability of nesting-spots
for all concerned.

On the lochan near the point were five whooper swans and a
few mallard. In the bay were many shags but little else. At
Rhu there was a blink of sunshine, the mist lifted, and an in-
vigorating warmth cheered us. The Cuillins cleared and in high
spirits we got back to the house.

In the dark, with snow falling, we left the glen. As we got to
Sligachan daylight was breaking and the snowy shadow of
Sgùrr nan Gillean solidifying out of the mist. New snow had
fallen in quantity in the night and as we sped down towards Kyle,
squalls blotted out the hills, clearing now and then to reveal pale
mountains against dark skies. Then the sun broke through to
touch everything with light and we were in a gilded isle of contrasting beauty, a beauty of soft greens and browns, snowy peaks
and illuminated stormclouds.

The mainland was deep in snow, and to Achnashellach,
through feathery pines and peaks of terraced snow walls that
loomed into an infinity of cloud was as wild a scene as anyone
could wish for. Mist and snow was the journey through the
Grampians to Glasgow.

But I have one complaint, and that is, that the great snow of which this was the first day, did not come one day sooner. If it had, I would not have been able to rejoin my unit, for Glen Brittle was cut off from the outside world for three weeks from the day I left. And there is a pair of skis in the house. But probably I am a glutton.

6

Wester Ross

"Somewhere few people go; somewhere wild and seldom visited where there are plenty of mountains and interesting birds; somewhere inaccessible. . . ." These were my thoughts as I turned over *Bartholomew's Atlas* in the Mitchell Library of Glasgow. I could think of many places but the map has a way of crystallizing things, the memory is stirred, and remembered views spring into focus recalling old intentions.

"The Fannichs!" Before my eyes floated a range of grey quartz peaks, vast and lonely, as I had seen them from the Torridon peaks years before. I had sworn to explore them some time. Eagerly I examined the map. South of the Dirre More, the Destitution Road, they lie linked together by high ridges. North of them was yet another range of peaks unsuspected by me, the Ben Dearg group, sufficient in all to last any one a long time. This was the place I wanted. All that required doing now was preparation.

It was my favourite time, early in May, when I set out. There had been a heat wave as I made my plans and counted the days. Now, new snow was on the Campsie Fells and the weather forecast promised unsettled wintry weather, a Buchan cold spell in fact. Nor was the sight of my gear reassuring. A friend had gifted me an old cycle with a twenty-six-inch frame that I could barely fit. On to its strengthened carrier my Bergan was tied, complete with projecting tent poles and photographic tripod. On my back was yet another rucksack; all this to make me self-supporting for at least nine days, when I hoped to be able to get more food.

I would have given a lot to cancel the whole project there and then but my pride forbade it. The Fannichs were bleak and cold in my imagination, and against their misty bulk I could see a little tent, inexpressibly lonely, whipped by lashing rain. I lifted my bike on to the road.

I have said I could barely fit the bike. Imagine the effort of

41

mounting. The frame was too tall for me to put my leg over, so what I had to do was run alongside the machine—taking good care to press my weight on the handlebars or the front wheel would shoot into the air because of the weight on the back— throw myself into the air, and keeping my leg out to avoid the tent poles, land with a bit of luck in the saddle. I may say I received a lot of encouragement from the local children before I mastered the technique necessary to take me to the station. It was a relief to see it in the guard's van.

Inverness was my destination—as far as the train went on the Sabbath—and in a smirr of rain whisked on a biting wind I bowled along the main street, thanking God when the traffic lights changed to green as I approached, for I had no method of descent save falling off. It was a bleak sort of a day and I pressed through the misty hills of Strathconnan, glad of the shelter of its trees, to swoop on my rocking steed down an exciting hill to Garve.

It was cold as I climbed up the desert of peat-hags which is the Dirre. Tibet could not have appeared more hostile than this empty land of dun bogs and mist-enshrouded snowy hills almost devoid of habitation. Then after ten miles of it, I came to pine trees and a little loch, Loch Droma, my destination. This was the spot I had picked on the map as a base-camp for my explorations. There was a house at the far end from which camping permission was readily forthcoming and under the lee of a wall I pitched my tent. With the tent door laced and the stove burning, it was cosy inside. I was glad I had come, the weather could do what it liked.

Flapping fabric and spraying rain awakened me in the night. One side of the tent had collapsed and fierce gusts buffeted it to and fro. The wind had shifted right round so that there was now no shelter. Quickly I got outside but the damage was not easily put right for the ground was stony and pegs would not go far down.

When I awoke again the skies were still pouring rain so I cooked breakfast and slept some more. The dazzle of the white tent brought me to consciousness. I leapt from my sleeping bag and looked out. Against a blue sky the whole Fannich range were glistening in the sunlight, brilliant in two thousand feet of new snow—deep snow too, by the look of it. Loch Droma with its green pines was a grand place indeed, the air was vital and already there was warmth in the sun. A hastily made sandwich and I was off.

Never in all my life have I gloried in a mountain view as in that from my first top, Meall a Chrasgaidh. Only those who have experienced the fullness of heart and pure bliss of mountains will understand my feelings. This was the first time I had been so far north by myself, and perhaps that added something to the intensity of feeling. Ringed round me were range upon range of dazzling mountains clear cut against the vivid sky. Down Strathmore was the blue cut of Loch Broom opening out to the Atlantic. There, to the north, was the fabled land of Sutherland, its isolated wedges snow-sharp over cloud-shadowed moors. South were the great ridges of piled mountains stretching away to the glens of Affric and beyond, Alpine chains indeed. From a hill loch a thousand feet below me came the piping of sand-pipers setting a kind of perfection to it all.

Sgùrr nan Clach Geala came next, a spade-shaped peak like Ben Lui, with beautiful north-east corries overhung with snow cornices that tapered away to delicate points in space. From it were views of my old friends, the Torridonian mountains, looking the last word in difficulty. But the peak that excited me most was An Teallach, a Cuillin ridge in itself, bristling with pinnacles set dizzily above the sea. And I would have the chance of climbing it!

Soft snow made the going heavy over Carn na Criche, the shapely Sgùrr Mór, and Beinn Liath Mhor Fannich, but I enjoyed the traverse all the more for it. In the light of a superb evening I dropped down the glen to my wee tent. Two eggs, a jug of milk, and some scones had been placed in the doorway—a kindly thought. Long after the sun set, the peaks still held its fire in afterglow. I was grateful to that wind that turned my tent over and brought fine weather.

Gold was stealing down the snows when I looked out on the following morning. Not one cloud was to be seen in the pale sky and from the woods came the intermingled songs of birds; grey wagtails flitted to and fro, obviously nesting near by; and for close company I had a robin and a wren, the loudest voiced wren I have ever met. The "drumming" of snipe was another fine sound to hear.

Ben Dearg, the highest peak north of the Garve–Ullapool road was my objective. As it is guarded by smaller peaks there are many ways of approach, but the one that appealed to me was by Loch a' Gharbhrain and Loch an Eilein. And it was a grand choice. Greenshank swooped at my head—the first I had ever seen—and on the lochs were nesting gulls and shoveller duck. I put up goosanders from the rivers too.

Above me, walled in by great crags was a corrie hanging with snow cornices, Ben Dearg to its left, to the right Cona Mheall. Excited at this unsuspected ferocity I scrambled up good crags flanking the great drop till all that remained was a plateau of scintillating snow crowned by an igloo which was the summit cairn.

Far below were the tiny houses of Ullapool, and away beyond Loch Broom was Lewis, a shadow on the sea. Wherever I looked there were mountains, all beckoning to be climbed. Immediately opposite me, the face of Cona Mheall seemed to drop in one vertical swoop to the floor of the corrie—an illusion—for later I descended it. The Sutherlandshire mountains seemed remarkably near, a sterile land that repelled rather than attracted me.

Two peaks, Meall nan Ceapraichean and Ceann Garbh, made a fine crossing before tackling the illusionary mountain. From its fierce top I was able to appreciate the full wildness of this tremendous corrie floored by the black loch from which it gets its name, Coire Ghranda. Two years later I was to experience a terrifying thunderstorm in that corrie, the walls acting as sounding-boards to echo the thunder crashes.

Mist and rain on a west wind was disheartening on the morning following but I had been lucky so I could not complain. At a loose end, I strolled up to the house for a chat with the friendly Mac-Kenzies. Kenny, the old man, was bemoaning the state of his bicycle. He wanted to go and cut some lambs but his ancient steed was punctured and the chain was loose.

Well, I had nothing to do, so I whipped a couple of links off the chain, repaired the puncture, oiled and adjusted the brakes, and asked him to try it out. He mounted stiffly, pedalled it up the road, turned round, and as he came free-wheeling past, his face was beaming and his mutton-chop whiskers flying in the wind. "Man, it's yourself is a grand enshineer," he shouted. That sealed our friendship. When I asked him if they were never lonely, just his wife and himself in such an out of the way place, he replied, "No, you see, we have the grand set of wireless." It was a delight to talk to him and hear his quaint Gaelic phrases. Never have I had greater kindness shown to me than from these old friends, Mr. and Mrs. MacKenzie. Alas, Kenny is dead now, and Mrs. MacKenzie no longer lives in the Highlands.

That night the wind backed to the east again, and sunset over the pinnacles of An Teallach, with a foreground of silhouetted pines and cloud lanes of different colours on Loch Droma, was a sight to remember. All night long the wading birds kept calling; mingling calls of piping oyster-catchers, whinnying curlews, plaintive redshanks, "ticking" and "drumming" snipe, "peeping" sandpipers, etc. This is a chorus I never tire of.

An Teallach I was reserving for a really fine day, and after another day on the Fannichs it came. It had been dull, but at midday cleared to a breezy day of fine visibility. The peak stood up better than ever before and down the glen I bashed on the old bike, sliding and slipping on the atrocious road. By a dip in the strata I ascended from the woods where I parked the bike, and if I had stopped to admire that wonderland of mountain and sea that opened up at every hundred feet I would be climbing yet. Glas Meall Mór was my first top, but better was ahead, so over this wonderful ridge I went, each peak an invitation and something of a rock scramble.

Corrag Bhudhe and its four fingers of rock sitting above Loch Toll an Lochain must be one of the finest seats in Scotland. Here above this tumult of Torridonian sandstone I watched the Minch turn to silver as the sun sank westwards purpling the big hills of Harris and the Cuillins of Skye. Below me was the Strath na Shellag and the shapely mountains that stretch in beautiful waves from Beinn Dearg Mhór to Slioch, a country I vowed I would explore some day. A steep snow gully took me from Sail Liath to the Lochan. The sandstone serrations of the tops were stained wine-red now against the paling sky, the snow edges of the gullies being exquisitely textured.

It was not until it came to cycling back to Loch Droma that I realized how tired I was. There are ten peaks on An Teallach, and the traverse involves a lot of retracing of steps. Also, on the hill I had eaten only a slice of brown bread which was all I had with me. Add to that fifteen miles, all of it uphill, and you will know I do not exaggerate when I say I could hardly turn the pedals when eventually I reached blessed camp. But a grand feed put me right. About three minutes in the sleeping bag and I was in the Land of Nod.

The sunshine streaming into the tent woke me on the morning following. It was ten-thirty but I had no shame as I felt I had earned a day off, and besides, I wanted to give a hand at the peats for all the kindness shown to me. Also, there were a lot of nests I wanted to visit.

That was a fine day. We cut peats, the three of us, Kenny doing the skilled part and Mrs. MacKenzie spreading them, I stacking them. In the evening we went out on the loch to fish. Kenny pulled them in good style and plied the landing-net while I landed a beauty. A very peaceful business, fishing.

Then came the finest day of all for weather, the Sabbath, and in all Kenny's years as a keeper he had never gone to the hill on the Sabbath. Also, Mrs. MacKenzie had planned a dinner for me. A dinner which I shall always remember, especially that rhubarb tart swamped in thick cream. But my heart was on the tops that day, and at half-past eight in the evening I asked Kenny if he had any objection to my going off to see the sunrise. He had not, and I set off, carrying only a sleeping bag. Down to Loch a' Bhraoin I cycled. Then began a marathon race with the sun, to see whether I would get on to the top of A' Chailleach in time to catch its last light. I won by a few minutes.

The whole west was a blaze of gold reaching to fire-tinted clouds, then pale lemon through amethyst to blue-green. Threads of silver traced the shadowy glens and each lochan was a splash of quicksilver, the lighting apparently being given from the sky. Cutting the gaudy clouds near at hand was the pinnacled silhouette of An Teallach, hard edged as though newly cut. Through a gap in the hills west of it lay Gruinard Bay on which a lighthouse flashed steadily. Away to the north another one flashed, a long flash and a short interval. I got into my sleeping bag and watched the grey tops melt into the night. Over the Fannich a tiny lantern of light was the edge of the waning moon.

Gradually the gold of the west shifted round the horizon. It was deathly still on top except for the roaring of the mountain torrents that seemed to emphasize the stillness. Perhaps I slept, anyway, I was suddenly aware of things taking shape again and of peaks that floated on clouds. I was on a cloud myself detached from the earth, and only the tops of the mountains, islands on a cloud sea, were visible.

The whole east was afire. Slowly the burning rim of the sun appeared, a speck growing every minute. All the clouds below me were tinted, and as I stood up at the wonder of it, a huge circle of rainbow, the width of the valley it seemed to me, was cast across the vapours at my feet. For a second it flickered brightly, then was gone. That was indeed a magic moment.

It was bitterly cold and over the ridge of Sgùrr Breac on hard frozen snow I walked. A little left of the quartz of Beinn Eighe and Liathach were five sharp peaks of purest blue, the Cuillin of Skye. Here on this happiest morning of my life, I heard for the first time the full song of a snow-bunting, a rare privilege indeed. All Scotland was mine that morning.

I stayed up there until the sun was warm and high in the sky before plunging into the gloom of the clouds. Six hours' sleep in the sunshine by the loch-side, for the clouds had dispersed as I descended, put me just right for an evening at the peat. I found it hard to believe it was all part of the same day.

Ben Wyvis seen from all my tops had looked worth climbing besides being celebrated for its view, so on the following day I cycled down to the house of Garbat and plodded up its steep grass on to An Cabar. Mist covered the Black Isle but in the west all was clear. Over fine turf by a wild corrie the traverse of the peaks went, seven tops in all.

But the best of the day came as I retraced my steps over the last top at sunset. An eagle was sunning itself on a rock projection overhanging the corrie. I had good cover and managed to get close to it for a spy through the glass. An incautious movement, and up went its head. From its perch the great bird dropped into space, opening its wings in the air. That was my first good view at close quarters of a golden eagle.

There is little left to tell. I climbed other peaks but I have dwelt only on the highlights. This was the first long holiday I spent by myself in the far north. It was a great and enriching experience, opening up a more satisfying way of mountain enjoyment than I had known in the past. I felt closer to nature and more at one with my environment. There was a fullness too in

the friendships I had made, and all the thrill of exploring new
country.

"Haste ye back," said Mrs. MacKenzie when I left them.
They stood at the door and watched me as I turned my bike
round the bend and faced the "Destitution Road".

7

Arran

PERHAPS it was because Arran was too near to hand; perhaps because so many people went to the island; perhaps because it meant devoting a whole holiday week-end when I could be farther afield. Anyway, it happened that of all the mountains that can be conveniently climbed from Glasgow, the Arran peaks were the only ones I had not explored.

It was too late at the railway station to bemoan my decision to go there. The day was "Fair Saturday", the day when all of Glasgow take themselves "doon the water". Indeed, all of Glasgow seemed to be trying to cram on to my train! I was crushed against the door, and all the way to Ardrossan prayed that the internal pressure would not burst it off its hinges.

That was the train. The boat could have been described as a seething mass of people, had there been room to seethe! Nevertheless, the folk were happy, and I felt less inclined to turn up my nose by the time the boat pulled in to Brodick. When the sun shines on "Fair Saturday" who can fail to be infected with the gay holiday spirit of Glasgow people? Besides, the mere sight of the granite peaks of Arran, scarred by rock and scree, and linked by high rugged ridges, was worth coming a long way.

I lost no time in Brodick and was soon heading round the bay, past the boarding-houses to where the track leads off up Glen Rosa. The heat was fierce and a plague of flies followed me as I toiled up the Rosa with my heavy bag. I intended to get as far out of range as possible of the rubber-neck tourist.

High up, under Beinn a' Chliabhain, I found a flattish bit of turf and on it I perched my tent. A can of tea and a bite to eat and I was soon trying a route on the rough rock of Cir Mhór, a route which defeated me, for I had yet to develop the special technique of Arran climbing. Nevertheless, I had grand sport and was thrilled at the ferocity of my immediate surroundings. I had never imagined such craggy steeps or true mountain effect. Far from being inferior hills, here were peaks fine as any outside

Skye, and with a variety of form second only to the Cuillin. The
"Witch's Step" looked to be like another "Inaccessible Pinnacle".

Along the summit ridge, over A' Chìr to Beinn Tarsuinn and
Beinn Nuis was a delightful scramble, of widening views, and
vistas of sea coasts and the mountainous island of Jura. Over
Beinn a' Chliabhain by steep slabs and long heather I came back
to camp. More exciting than the climbing or the views was the
fact that I had seen no human being since coming up the glen.
This was a discovery.

Wind and rain lashed down all the next morning, but, as it
does so often in Arran, the weather cleared in the afternoon and
I climbed that grand section of ridge from Goatfell to Cioch na
h-Oighe. The plunging buttresses of the latter peak and the views
over the Firth to the Highland hills were all I asked for. My
camp, with its view to Cìr Mhór and the tooth of Ceum na
Caillich, seemed a delightful spot that clear evening.

Reluctantly I left next morning for the early boat. Not until
I joined the main road did I meet a living soul, so my illusions
of Arran as a place crawling with people were well and truly
shattered. I had been neglecting a great little island.

I was to get to know Arran well in the years that followed.

North Sannox Bay was a favourite camping site of mine, a
green fringe of turf on the edge of the sea, sheltered by woods
which in spring were loud with singing birds. Through the gap
carved out by the mountain torrent which cleaves the bay you
can see the jagged rocks riding the sky high above the gorge.

From the tent door I have watched that dainty little orange-
billed bird, the ringed plover, search the stones for food. Oyster-
catchers, redshanks, and curlews sound continuously, and out to
sea gannets are always wheeling and diving. Red-throated divers
come close inshore and mergansers are very fond of sleeping on
the stones. A redstart used to have a perch on the stone wall
that supported my guy ropes. Sometimes it was joined by a
spotted flycatcher and they would have a flycatching competition. No corner of Skye has more appeal for me than this little
bit of pure island scenery. I used to start the day bird-watching, and, after a climb, finish it the same way.

Nor must I forget the Beinn Bharrain group, the Red Cuillin
of Arran, as different in character from the main ridge as the
Black Cuillin from the Red. Here are rounded hills with wild

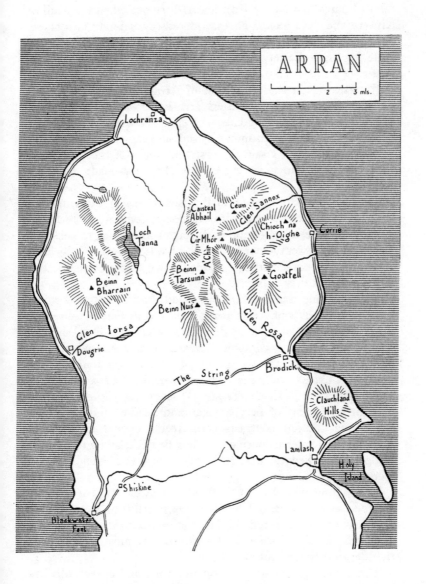

ARRAN

1   2   3 mls.

Lochranza

Loch
Tanna

Caisteal
Abhail

Ceum
Glen Sannox

Chioch na
h-Oighe

Corrie

Cir Mhór

A'Chir

Beinn
Tarsuinn

Beinn
Bharrain

Goat Fell

Beinn Nuis

Glen Iorsa

Glen Rosa

Dougrie

The String

Brodick

Clauchland
Hills

Lamlash

Holy
Island

Shiskine

Blackwater
Foot

glens separating them. I shall never forget the October day on Beinn Bharrain, a day of frost and rich colour when the Mull of Kintyre and Jura looked an easy step away. A day memorable for the ribbon of black geese that flew in a noisy gaggling throng quite low over the top: the first geese of winter down from the Arctic.

That season on the west coast of Arran was full of interest, for each day brought new bird arrivals. Past the cave where Bruce is said to have watched the spider I used to walk from Shiskine, by cliffs of cormorants, rock-doves, and great throngs of noisy jackdaws. I saw the first turnstones of the year there, hosts of duck, and a variety of wild life that made each day a thrill.

But my outstanding visit to the island was in the winter of 1942. I was weary of train travel, having come up from Dover through a succession of air-raids that turned the fifteen-hour journey into a twenty-four hour one. I was determined to climb, and on a cold dark morning plodded down to St. Enoch Station for the eight-thirty train.

That morning was a reward to the faithful. Rose-tinted clouds were over the hills of Arran when I arrived in Fairlie. Over the ridge above the town a golden glow was spreading, showing where the sun was climbing. West, pinnacle after pinnacle thrust themselves through the clouds, their tops touched with sunlight. The sail over the blue sea crested with sparkling foam was exhilarating in the frosty air. At length the Cumbraes hove in sight, with tints of fiery bracken and heather and grey rocks that made autumn contrasts seem feeble compared with this brilliance of winter colouring. At last Brodick, and a bus run by golden beech hedges, past little bays busy with sheldrake and mergansers, to Corrie.

Mrs. Hunter of Heathfield made me welcome, despite my unexpected arrival, and I lost no time in getting off to the hill, up over the frozen hill-side to the punchbowl of Cioch na h-Oighe. By fairly steep iced rocks for the most part, I made the top and stepped into sunshine.

The sun was level with me on the ridge and every gully and scree slope across Glen Sannox was ablaze with mellow light that made jewels of every rock fragment. The Firth was calm and serene, floating its sombre islands before the snowy bulk of the

Highland hills. With the setting sun gilding the western peaks I trod the ridge over to Goatfell. Till dusk I sat on the top, and as the deeper shadow of night dimmed the bays and glens, I made my way to the house, running the slopes with that elation of movement that is given to the happy hillman.

A starry morning. To the east, a long line of low fire-tinted clouds. The shore-lines, curving silhouettes cutting a wonderful pattern of interweaving lanes of dark but luminous colour which is the sea. That was the morning when I got out the car at Glen Rosa.

The larches were a brown haze in the frozen glen. As I gained height on Beinn Nuis the first touch of flame lit Cìr Mhór. The effect on this pinnacle was spectacular, a red wedge of rock in a green sky. Gradually the warm light stole from top to top, glistening on ice and snow and bringing life to the gullies and screes. Brittle with intense light, these peaks had the majesty of the Cuillin that morning.

I made for the hollow of Nuis, already a suntrap marvellously inviting below its pale cloudless sky. To scramble on its red-grey rocks on such a morning was the peak of living. Ravens barked and tumbled overhead, and a fierce encounter with a pair of eagles showed that they had thoughts of nesting in their heads.

Suddenly, out of nothing, a mist formed, a scarf of silky vapour thrown over the peak. I was above it as it twisted, and Holy Isle, seen as a fragment of peak above a sparkling lochan, was as mighty as the peak of Clach Glas.

The crossing to A' Chir this vital morning was annoying. Ice defeated me on practically all the little rock routes, usually just as I was congratulating myself on success. From A' Chir I went over Caisteal Abhail and on to the "Witch's Step". Here, on this finger of rock, so well guarded by its peculiar little difficulties to-day set with ice, I sat to watch the sunset. Again Cìr Mhór was the favoured peak. The last sun threw a shaft of vivid purple, gold-edged and shimmering, across its cleft top. Only a moment it lasted and then was gone, leaving the great face dark.

The floor of Sannox was as slippery as an ice-rink when I got down to it in darkness. It was good to get in that night after such a good day, and feel at home in the sitting-room of my old friends.

Thereafter, blizzards and gales swept the peaks, and waves broke over the island roads with a crashing din that was frightening. It is always thus with the weather in the west. If a "super day" comes with a breath-taking brilliance of colour, make the most of it, for you are almost certainly in for a bad spell afterwards.

But I did not regret those wild days when I was nearly blown off the tops and half frozen for the effort. It was just another manifestation of nature and another sidelight on a truly fine little island.

8

Ben Nevis

*. . ., however happiness may
shun pursuit, it may nevertheless be sometimes
surprised basking on the weird granite crags.*

A. F. MUMMERY

It was the Scottish Mountaineering Club's guide-book to Ben Nevis that fired my young ambitions. I would climb the Tower Ridge. It sounded good and was of sufficient length to meet my enthusiastic demands. An uncomfortable night at two thousand feet, defying gravity in a single blanket on a steep slope was my preparation. It had seemed romantic this sleeping-out part, but I had been caught in darkness before I could select a flat place. Anyway, the bitter cold itself would have prevented sleep and killed the romance, so the diversion of preventing myself from rolling to the foot of the mountain was probably an advantage.

Early morning saw me traversing above the lochan into the corrie. The sun was shining but I could not quell a vague fear of what was to come, for above me the rocks rose steeper and steeper. Never had I seen such an unfriendly-looking place. High against the sky the pinnacles and edges of red rock showed what had to be climbed before the top could be gained. I shuddered to think of climbing up there all alone with that terrible drop below me. I stood below the Douglas Boulder and looked upwards. Two thousand feet of rock above me was the top of the Ben. I had not the heart to even attempt it. I felt something of a failure that night when I came down off Càrn Dearg.

Not for ten years did I come back to the Ben, to stroll up from Glen Nevis, cut a few steps near the top, and see the beautiful ice decorations of the heavily corniced ridge. Traversing round to Càrn Dearg over the arête, the full splendour of that north-east face burst on me with a new impact. The whole thing looked impossible and a kind of climber's nightmare of verticality.

I spoke to my old friend Drummond Henderson about it. "Do you mean to tell me you have never done a climb on the Ben?" he demanded. I confessed my ignorance. "Well, you let me know the next time you get leave and we will see what can be arranged. If it is in the spring so much the better."

So on April 21, 1945, I arrived in Fort William to keep the tryst. I had come from Skye where there was new snow on the Red Hills and a briskness in the air that suggested more to come. Drummie was not due to arrive till evening so I spent the afternoon enjoying the bustle of this busy little town, and later climbing Cow Hill for its celebrated view of the Ben. The green of the glen with its snowy peaks edging the blue sky made me impatient to be off.

Drummie arrived on the late train and it was good to get his crack, as always, well spiced with humour. It was late before we committed ourselves to our respective grooves in the double bed.

Our hopes of a good day were fulfilled and in sunshine we walked round to the distillery, complete with rope and ice-axes. A cuckoo was calling, exceptionally early for this part of the country, and among the birches there were redpolls and a willow warbler. High up in the Allt a' Mhuilinn we chose a sunny nook among a nest of boulders and there spent a happy half-hour eating sandwiches and enjoying the warmth. Above us rose the edge of the "castle ridge", and on the skyline was the "northeast buttress". Ice sparkled on the upper rocks, and there was a fair smattering of fresh snow. A pair of eagles circled the blue sky on great black wings.

We pushed to the hut and brewed coffee, sipping it outside in the warmth while Drummie pointed out to me the wonders of this inner chamber, a chamber of contrasting red rocks, glistening snow, and long shadowy gullies dark with ice: "the trident", "tower ridge", "observatory ridge", numbers 2, 3, 4 and 5 gullies, "ledge route", "Slav wall", Coire na Ciste, the latter a place where Drummie would dearly spend the day were greater matters not afoot. No man has a greater love of the Ben than he.

"Now, if I had to introduce some one to the Ben, and all they could spare was one day of their lives, I would go for the

CENTRAL HIGHLANDS

4   8 mls

Ardgour

Glen Nevis

Ben
Nevis

Aonach
Mór

Aonach
Beag

Loch
Treig

Mamore Forest

Blackwater Reservoir

LOCH

LINNHE

Aonach Eagach

Bidean
nam
Bian

Lairig Eilde

Buachaill Beag

Buachaill Etive Mór

Kingshouse

RANNOCH

MUIR

Clachlet

Stob Coir'an
Albannaich

Stob
Ghabhar

Beinn
Starbh

Meall nan
Eun

Loch
Tulla

Glas
Bheinn
Mhór

Loch
Etive

Bridge of
Orchy

Oban

Cruachan

'Observatory ridge'," said Drummie. "Look how it rises in a thin wedge from the foot of the corrie right to the summit." I followed his finger. "The gullies on either side are unclimbable too, so there is no escape once committed to it."

"Do you think it is possible?" I asked, thinking of the ice and new snow on the upper steeps. "It may be," said Drummie, "but I'll leave it to you to decide, for you are going to have the honour of leading."

With some trepidation I tied on the rope and led upwards. What a glorious climb! Steep rock led us to the truly grandiose in rock scenery. And the climbing was always delightful, with the country of Knoydart opening out at every upward step. Then we got on to real ice and snow. Step cutting and clearing rocks, we were in our element, and there was always the uncertainty as to whether our route was passable or not. The full exposure of the climb was rock-climbing at its very best. "Get over the next bit and we are up," said Drummie. And sure enough, a steep wall leading to a snow arête and we were up.

Happily we trod the summit and revelled in the views. North of where a wild tangle of purple hills threw themselves against the golden rays of the setting sun, were the Cuillins of Skye and Rúm, faint but distinct. Far north were the snows of the Monar hills, beautifully clear and delicately tinted. South, Bidean nam Bian and the Glen Coe hills to Ben More and Stobinian. Near at hand were the Mamores, flushed to a rare brilliance of contrast between grey, russet, and green.

We stayed up there for a long time, examining the huge snow cornices and bulges of overhanging ice that crowned the upper rocks. The "Gardiloo" gully was in the fiercest condition Drummie had ever known it. Looking down from the top of the Ben to the dizzy depths of the Allt a' Mhuilinn, it was hard to believe we had come up that way.

Reluctantly we left the top, a trifle, but not unduly, chilled, for the air was reasonably still. In the blaze of the sun's last fling we ran down the vivid green slopes, a welcome change after snow and rock. Drummie sang a few Gaelic songs. Fort William was as still as a Highland town on the Sabbath should be, when we got in at ten p.m., having been away from the hotel just over twelve hours.

All too soon came morning. To quote some one whom I have

forgotten: "What a day for a man who loves the Highlands to be leaving them!" That journey south was the finest in my experience. From that grand viewpoint between Fort William and Spean Bridge, Ben Nevis was tremendous, curving from green to brown, then to dark cleaving crags reaching to jagged scars of red rock that thrust from dazzling snow edges.

The Mamores, too, enthralled, each peak seeming new in its present rebirth of spring life. All the familiar things were at their best: Loch Treig; the blue lochans of Rannoch; the Glen Coe peaks, giant seeming, across the moor; Loch Tulla and the beautiful Starbh group; Loch Lomond and its trees a wealth of green life; Loch Long, a thin slit, with old man Cobbler bent above it.

Yes, that was a journey to remember. It is worth while neglecting a fine mountain if the remaking of the friendship has so much to offer.

9

Glen Cannich

THE central glens! There was a rich harvest of "Munros" to
reap (a peak over three thousand feet is known as a "Munro" in
Scotland), and the natural forests of old birches held promise of
all sorts of things in the world of birds. And the lochs, Affric,
Mullardoch, Monar, buried among the remote hills, had the
thrilling sounds of places where ospreys might lurk. The whole
area from Strath Bran to Glen Morrison had occupied my fancy
for long, and I felt the time was come to do something about it.

I wrote to the postmistress at Beauly and found I could get
by mail-car well into any of these dead-end glens. I wrote also
to the lodge marked "Benula" on the map, asking for accommodation since I wanted to travel light, but without success. The
keeper was forbidden to accommodate climbers, even though
the month was May and there was no prospect of sport for yet
another three months.

However, I hit on a plan. I sent up parcels of food in my
own name marked "To be called for", and travelled up by the
mail-car through the beautiful pines and inspiring river scenery
of Strath Glas to Glen Affric Hotel where I changed cars for the
bumpy ride up to Benula.

Among groves of sun-brilliant birches clustering in the gullies and
growing out of the hill-sides at every angle, was the entrance to
my chosen glen, Glen Cannich. Loch Mullardoch was a wilder
spot and when we got to Benula I thought it a bleak spot indeed, a
place of peat bogs and grey clouds pressing down on the mountains.

The keeper was a kindly young fellow and offered to put me
up now that I was there. But there was little point in perhaps
getting him into trouble with his possessive "Laird", so I sought
for a camping spot and found a nice little place half a mile off
on the edge of a pine wood. I was tired with all-night travel and
glad to have a meal and snuggle into my sleeping-bag, the
flapping canvas conveying a cosy feeling of well-being.

See Strathfarrar map, page 114.

I awoke to the shrilling of greenshank and the loud piping of oyster-catchers. My holiday had indeed started. Not a breath of wind stirred and the green hills around me were overdrawn by a grey line of settled clouds. There was no knowing what the day would bring forth, so I had a leisurely breakfast, picking up my binoculars now and then to watch a sandpiper or red-shank go about its business. From the wood came songs of blackbirds and thrushes, and the little chorus of wrens and willow warblers thrown in made a lovely little choir.

There had been a drought for eight weeks I was told, so deciding that it would hardly break the day of my arrival, I set off for the peak Beinn Fhionnlaidh, disturbing a ptarmigan from its seven eggs *en route*. Carn Eighe came next, a peak with a name that has always fascinated me. To-day it was just an-other misty mountain. I took a bearing to Mam Sodhail and as I left the top the clouds broke open. Blue peaks leapt out of the north and south. With a thrill I recognized the spire of Liathach and the Torridon mountains. Sgorr na Cìche of Knoydart, an-other old friend, was unmistakably recognizable, and I could see the sunshine on Ben Nevis, the scorings of its cliffs quite visible. I was massed round with ridges and tangled up in peaks and deep glens, a bewildering effect as the mist flirted with this new mountainland of mine.

In these dramatic mists I gained Mam Sodhail's summit, and taking advantage of the openings hurried over that grand ridge to Sgùrr na Lapaich. Despite the height, the air was inert and charged with a feeling of expectancy. Even the moving clouds were curiously lifeless, their grey-black movements having some-thing rather sinister about them.

A lot of retracing of steps, my "Munro"-bagging instinct prompting me to take in my stride various little tops, made the journey back quite hard going. The first rain fell as I reached the tent. The drought had broken, and for the next thirty hours it was hopeless to even think of climbing.

Showers and bright sunshine and I was glad to quit a pro-longed sloth in the flea-bag for the heights of An Raibhachan. The weather-man must have had a chuckle when he saw me, compass in hand and well and truly soaked, feel my way across this complicated ridge to the real Sgùrr na Lapaich. Yes, there are two of them, almost opposite each other. Sitting up there, cold and wet, with nothing to see but mist and the prospect of nothing else but mist, I reflected that in such conditions mountains are a physical extravagance and climbing a mere dissipation of energy.

However, despite these ruminations, yet another two "Munros" were to be had for the taking if I was willing to face a rather big drop. It is good to be young and stupid, for five hundred feet down I was in sunshine, and from the heights of Creag Dubh I sat comfortable, a feast of colour round me, from the purple of the Fannichs of Ross, by Loch Monar and Torridon, round and down south to the gauzy blues of Glen Shiel and beyond. The beauty of that evening; the sudden switch from bleak winter to warm summer; the glen of birches gay and green; and the evening birdsong was my dream of hills at their best. Life was good that evening.

Now, my off-time when the weather was bad had not been completely wasted. Two nests in suitable places for photography intrigued me—those of a sandpiper and a tree creeper. I had made little hides to assist me in the job, and with the help of the keeper's housekeeper I was ready to begin work on the tree creeper the following morning.

The birds took no notice of the hide, and I had some good fun watching these mouse-like little things. Their nest was behind the peeling bark of an old pine-post used as a stake and my first job was to patch the affair with string for the wind swayed it almost to collapse. What fun I had that morning!

Often the two birds were at the nest together, spiralling and making thin squeaking noises for all the world like excited mice. Once I saw the hen, presumably, take food from the cock and give it in a lovely little movement to the young. It is a peculiar example of instinct that the nestlings associate sound with food for my finger thrust into the nest evoked no response, yet I needed only to touch the bark where the parents climbed to reach the nest, and every bill would spring open.

Once too, I averted what might have been a tragedy. Two ends of a great fat grub were left sticking out of the gullet of a youngster and despite heaving gulps of its quilly little body, it could not swallow them. Thinking it might choke, I caught the protruding ends and lifted the youngster out of the nest before the grub came away. I noted that rather large grubs were assisted down the gullets of the offspring by stabs of the parent bill.

The sandpiper proved a shy subject and, fearing it would desert, I abandoned it, making instead for the peak Toll Creagach and a ridge traverse of the tops to Carn Eighe, my peak of a few days ago. I had sleet, rain and snow on the tops, but fine mist effects too. Bedraggled and ready for a feed I got back to the tent. The kindly folks of Benula had inserted eggs and milk and scones in my absence so I had a royal repast.

At three p.m. next day there was a strange silence in the tent. The rain was off. The sun came forth, so feeling favoured indeed, I set off for An Socach above Loch Lungard. All the freshness of spring was in the caller air that afternoon of wet green hills and fleeting cloud.

On top the weather was not so settled. To the west was the Minch lit by slanting sunrays out of which towered—towered is the only word—the rain-blurred hills of the Red Cuillin. Due north to Torridon and Monar the peaks were blackly outlined against a clear patch of sky above which hung rainclouds. A joyful day to be on the hill.

Now I had left the tit-bit to the last, a beautiful mountain with an unpronounceable name—Sgùrr nan Ceathreamhnan. Its position and height of 3,736 feet is bound to make it a great view-point so I particularly wanted a good day for it. Also it is, by reason of numerous ridges, a difficult mountain in mist. To climb it from where I was camped meant a long day which was another reason for wanting good weather for it. But my days were down to one, so next day I had to take pot-luck.

The morning was showery, and feeling optimistic, I made myself up a parcel of sandwiches, an especially big parcel for I knew I would be gone a long time. At the last moment I decided to take a rucksack and into it went my camera, gloves, etc. The walk up was stimulating for there was every chance of a good day.

I had just reached the base of my first peak when down came the rain. And it lashed the whole time I was on the tops. On the first peak I found an overhanging boulder and under it un-packed my rucksack for a bite to eat. With a shock I found I had left my food in the tent. This was serious, for hunger can make you very weak on hills, as I well knew. Anyway, I decided to go on and in a snow blizzard traversed six of the tops and felt quite conceited to have accomplished them. I felt no ill effects from the lack of food except a hunger that, when satisfied, kept me awake all night.

Next day was a problem. I had arranged to meet an old friend, Frank Nelson, at a spot on the map called Crowe Bridge, Loch Duich. We had fixed on four p.m., and to be sure of getting there in time, I had banked on leaving camp in the morning, knocking half the walk off that day, leaving the other half for the remaining time. Now it was sheeting it down, and to even think of walking seemed the height of stupidity.

The walk was considerable with my weight of luggage, for I had two hill passes to cross and I know enough of hill paths to be wary of dotted lines on the map. Nevertheless, I decided to stay put for the day, and making an early start next morning, push on in the hope of getting there by the arranged time.

Getting up at four a.m. was bad enough, but the weather quite put the finishing touches to it. The rain was even heavier than yesterday. I left the tent standing and stepped out into the elements, bound for Glen Affric. I went by Gleann a' Choilich, which comes down into the wildest part of Affric. At fifteen hundred feet on the *bealach* I was in snow, snow up to the ankles, the path being obliterated in places. On the summit at 2,300 feet the scene was so wintry—wind, hurrying snowflakes, and mist—that it was impossible to believe the month was May.

I was glad to reach the lonely house of Altbeath and get shelter out of the cold and wet for a cup of tea. This isolated house had its own school and teacher for the children and I was sorry to leave its cheery company for the pass to Glen Lichd.

What a pass is Glen Lichd! Set with foaming torrents and enclosed by the "Five Sisters" to the south, and the bulk of Beinn Fhada to the north, it is a place of savage grandeur. That day, waterfalls poured in wild spate over its numerous ravines, and above them the peaks loomed gigantic in their snowy summits. The thunder of wind and water was nature's musical accompaniment to such a wilderness.

At four p.m. I had still a couple of miles to do, when rounding a bend, I saw a lithe figure coming towards me. It was Frank. He had motored up from Carlisle and had in fact arrived only half an hour before me. So our arrangement had worked. It

was now a fine afternoon and Loch Duich from the Mam
Rattagan road had Frank speechless with admiration.

We camped at Glen Elg that night on a beautiful green spot
gay with sea-pinks. Over the water was the Scùir of Eigg, deep
blue in the soft sunshine. From the tent door, on the glossy
surface of the sea we could watch red-throated divers, mergansers,
and eider ducks. The air was balmy and we strolled around in
shirt sleeves.

I wondered if I was imagining things when I thought of the
wild country I had traversed and of the whirling snows of that
morning.

10

Kintail

To persuade Matt to go to Skye that year was a mistake, as I realized our first day out, a day when the gloom of the Cuillin was a shroud on the enthusiasm of even the keenest follower of the craft.

Why I insisted on such a remote spot as Coire an Lui and the central gully I shall never know either, for a more difficult place to find in mist in all the Cuillin would be hard to choose. I knew that after a lot of up and down work on the roughest of hill-sides and a few false starts on what looked like rock gullies.

Matt was taciturn. He became really bad-tempered when after three difficult and streaming wet pitches we were faced with an impasse, a bulging waterfall. This time there was no mistaking his true feelings or seeking to impose on his will. Waterlogged and disgruntled we got back to Glen Brittle. The rains looked permanent.

They were permanent.

Matt never recovered from that first day. He led a new route on Sròn na Cìche, climbed on Sgùrr nan Gillean, the Dubhs, etc., but all the time I knew he was not enjoying himself.

He is a man of few words, Matt, so when he said, "For God's sake let's find the sun," I knew he meant it. Next day saw us on the boat for Kyle. A mail-car marked "Shiel Bridge" seemed an indication of fate so we let things take their course, bought some food, and by Dornie Ferry and Loch Duich we came to Glen Shiel.

Matt was a new man. He sang Gaelic songs, even laughed a little, and despite the mist that was low over the glen, he gloried in the rich greens of the strath and contrasted it with the gloom of Glen Brittle. Beautiful turf invited camping, and on a bend of the river, three miles up, we pitched the tent. The air was calm and tints of sunset were on the clouds. "A good day to-morrow," said Matt. Verily his optimism had returned.

It was not a good day. We set off in rain and steered a

66

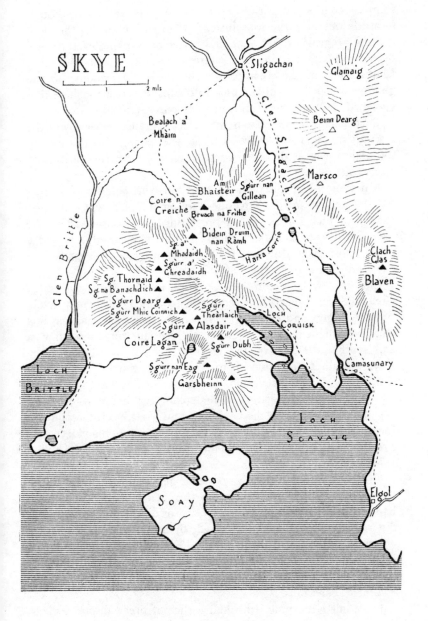

SKYE

1 mls   2 mls

Sligachan

Glamaig

Bealach a'
Mhàim

Beinn Dearg

Glen Sligachan

Marsco

Am
Bhaisteir   Sgurr nan
Gillean

Coire na
Creiche

Bruach na Frithe

Bidein Druim
nan Ràmh

Harta Corrie

Sg. a'
Mhadaidh

Clach
Glas

Sgurr a'
Ghreadaidh

Blaven

Sg. Thormaid
Sg. na Banachdich

Sgurr Dearg

Sgurr Mhic Coinnich

Sgurr
Theàrlaich   Loch
Corùisk

Sgurr Alasdair

Coire Lagan

Sgurr Dubh

Camasunary

Loch
BRITTLE

Sgurr nan Eag

Garsbheinn

Loch
SCAVAIG

Elgol

Glen Brittle

SOAY

compass course across the "Five Sisters". It was grand though to stride out over the tops instead of to rock-climb in the slow chilling progress of wet weather. "Give me walking every time," declared Matt, and in such circumstances I agreed with him. Matt's faith in the weather was justified. Descending to the glen we stepped out of the mist into sunshine, real sunshine that glistened on every rock and gully of our surroundings.

To go about camp that night in our shirtsleeves enjoying the warmth was to feel like "wild birds, that change their season in the night", except that we had gone one better by doing it in an afternoon.

A dry morning, misty on the tops but with patches of blue in the sky and gleams of sunshine lighting the glen was a definite change of luck for us. That great ridge, the south wall of the glen that runs to Cluanie, seemed from the map a high-level ridge of the most delightful sort, for the contours rose close and steep over top after top.

Into this wild region we went, to wander from Sgùrr na Creiche, over the Saddle, and out to Sgùrr Leac nan Each, Sgùrr na Sgne, and Foachag. Shifting mists and clear air gave us what we sought in views, views of tremendous ridges, north, east and south. West sharp and clear as needles were the Cuillin. I was afraid to mention them, but as we watched the sunset shifting west, Matt reflected, "It must be fine on the Cuillins to-night." "Coire Lagain must be looking real bonny right now," I said. "Trouble with the Cuillins," said Matt, "is they spoil you for other hills. Grassy hills feel tame, even good hills like these." From which I judged that Matt was sorry he had left the Cuillin. I know I was.

Our food situation was by no means good, and when we shifted our camp another seven miles up the glen towards Cluanie we had an idea that we were, literally, in for a thin time of it. That did not seem to matter very much then. Here were two fools whom experience had not taught. The number of peaks on the map seemed of more importance than such a prosaic thing as bodily nourishment. In the absence of rock we had become "Munro" conscious.

On a misty morning, with half a slice of bread in our pockets, we headed up to Druim Shionnach and Creag a Mhaim. There was no movement in the pressing clouds, and by compass we

The wildest shore of Loch Lomond with the Ben Lui mass dominating.

Strathfillan and the peaks of Ben More and Stobinian.

Rock climbing on the south peak of the Cobbler.

The crest of the Cuillin looking to Loch Coruisk from Sgurr Sgumain.

Relaxing on the gabbro shore of Loch Coruisk.

Approaching the south summit of Sgurr a Mhadaidh on the Cuillin ridge.

Loch Quoich before hydro-electrification developed it into a large reservoir.

From Sgurr na Ciche looking towards the Isle of Eigg.

Snow cornices, Sgor Mor Fannich, Wester Ross.

The summit ridge of An Teallach, Wester Ross.

Looking down on the head of Loch na Shellag. It is a roadless country in the remotest wilderness area of Scotland.

The view from Ben More Coigach to Loch Broom and Ben Dearg and the Fannich ranges.

Ullapool on Loch Broom, Wester Ross.

Loch Benevean in Glen Affric where paths lead to Kintail.

The Five Sisters of Kintail from Mam Ratagan pass.

Loch Duich and the peaks of Kintail.

The self-timer on the camera snaps Tom Weir at Loch Maree as he embarks northward for Sutherland, via the house of Carn More.

The lonely house of Carn More in its inhabited days. Stalker Calum Macrae is working at the peats in May.

Andy and Calum Macrae with Tom Weir in the middle. The boys were at work repairing the deer stalking path.

Camping at Lochnadamph in Sutherland. Matt looks out on a fine morning with cumulus breaking over Quinag.

Matt Forrester and Tom Weir after a rock climb getting to the top of Quinag. Looking towards the peaks of the Reay Forest.

Sutherland, and the green fields of Scourie with Handa Island in the background.

Climbing pals Frank Nelson and Matt Forrester at the Wells of Dee on the summit plateau of Braeriach around 4000ft. in June.

Lairig Ghru pass from the highest pines. The granite lies ahead.

At the Shelter Stone of Ben Macdhui in the mid 1950s. Clockwise: Tom Weir, George Roger, Matt Forrester, Ian McNicol and Percy McFarlane.

Loch Hournhead. There is no road beyond although paths lead in many directions into wild places.

Arnisdale, where the road ends at Corran. Ladhar Bheinn lies beyond, with Loch Hourn between.

The summit ridge of Liathach looks more difficult than it proves to be.

The late John Scobbie of Loch Stack, most delightful of keepers and good friend to the author.

Superlative Glen Coe and its 'Three Sisters', gashed by glens giving access to high tops like Stob Coire nan Lochan 3,657ft. shown here.

The Bidian nam Bian massif with Garbh Bheinn over a cloud sea on a crisp autumn day.

trotted over Aonoch air Chrith dutifully traversing all the tops to Sgorr an Lochain. Our half-slices of bread had been eaten, and in the absence of more spiritual food in the shape of views, etc., to take our minds off our inward cravings, we were on the point of descending when, like the prow of some great ship, a peak cleft the clouds, rolling them back in foamy breakers.

Our peak was suddenly isolated, the great cloud rollers submerging to steamy depths. From them rose new seas of mountains, seas delicate afar off, but near at hand vivid with sparkling rocks and russet facings. The wrinkled crags of Ben Nevis and the quartzy Mamores were marvellously near.

Hunger had gone. Creag na Damh was the last peak on our ridge and on to it we clambered to spend an hour on its summit. One of the most glorious hours of my life, an hour surrounded by the most beautiful country in all Scotland—south to Knoydart, north to Glen Affric, west to Rùm and the Cuillin, and east to the cleft of Glen Moriston.

"To sleep is to eat," is an old saying, and we proved its worth, for all we could afford to eat on our return was the other half of our respective slices.

Morning brought with it a heat-wave. In shorts and shirt sleeves we climbed Carn Fuarlach and Aonoch Meadhoin. The hills were trembly with steamy vapour drawn from the sodden earth.

Great biting clegs and the boiling sunshine made more a labour of the climb than a pleasure, thereby turning our minds inwards to thoughts of filling the gap. We finished up by walking the twelve miles to Ratagain Youth Hostel and making a raid on the Warden's store. I have happy memories of soup, more soup, and tinned fruit and milk. You can't beat a good starving if you want to enjoy your food!

The "Black Dog" descended on Matt next day. Maybe it was sunburn, maybe starvation, maybe too many hills for we had taken no days off and our stock of "Munros" had gone up considerably since leaving Skye. Whatever it was, he wanted to return home. I talked him into getting off the train at Fort William for an assault on Ben Nevis.

We did not get beyond our camping spot in the glen. The heat was terrific and Matt was already badly burnt.

"A mug's game," said Matt as we boarded the train next day

for home. "What pleasure is there in it? Starving yourself, knocking your pan in for nothing. Far better to have a fortnight down the Clyde; good grub; bags of rest; and the weather does not make or break you."

I permitted myself a quiet smile. That was eleven years ago and Matt still climbs, indeed he is keener now than I have ever known him.

Nor is it the first time he has recalled, "Do you remember that night on Creag na Damh when the mist cleared. . . ?"

11

In Wilder Ross

IF you examine the map of Ross, you will notice on the other side of Loch Maree from the tourist's shore, a tangle of steep contours distorted by dark shading and cut by numerous slashes of blue. The dark shading means rock, and the blue, of course, indicates lochs and lochans—an entrancing combination.

Years ago I stood on the top of Slioch, the Ben Lomond of Loch Maree, and looked over that wilderness of rock peaks bounded on the west side by An Teallach and on the east by the Fannich mountains. No roads traverse all this area and the shapely inaccessible peaks fired my imagination. As far as I knew, it was as virgin as the top of Mount Everest. No one of my acquaintance had been there or had even mentioned its existence. I vowed one day I would explore it.

The second week in May I found myself with seventeen days to spare. This was the opportunity. I planned to establish a base camp at Poolewe, and travelling reasonably light, make three- and four-day expeditions into the great unknown. It was a Saturday when I arrived in this lovely little village.

The postman, with whom I left my spare food and baggage, shook his head when I told him of my intention. He was still more horrified when he heard I was leaving on Sunday. "No good can come of climbing on the Sabbath," he told me. "And in this cold, changeable weather! Leave it until Monday if you must go." But I was anxious to be off, and with a lightly loaded Bergan containing sleeping-bag, tent, groundsheet, stove, cooking pans and food, waved him good-bye, telling him I would be back in the middle of the week. At last I was afoot towards my goal.

It was a bracing morning of clouds and intermittent sunshine as I threaded my way towards the great hills. Ahead was the boulder-strewn moorland that foots Beinn Airidh Charr. Soon I was under the sweeping rock wall of that mountain, each step of my track bringing new vistas of wild mountain form. Frogs splashed in the pools and their jellies glittered in the peat hags. Suddenly I came to a little lochan. Amongst the blue of the butterwort flowers I had half an hour by its shore. For music there were willow-warblers tinkling their little songs and sandpipers "wheeting".

That wonderful feeling of anticipation was on me as I headed the Fionn Loch under the steep crags of Beinn Làir. A camping spot was what I wanted now for time was getting on and I was keen to get on to a peak before dark. At last a little square of green in the water-logged moor invited. I did not realize how the wind had risen until I unpacked my one-man tent and struggled with its flapping canvas. Those who have pitched a tent solo will understand. My tent looked very lonely "in that oasis of perpendicularity".

A light meal and I was off for A' Mhaighdean across the causeway between Fionn Loch and Dubh Loch. The rock starts low down on this peak and in no time I was scrambling on delightfully sound stuff. This is what I had come for. A full appreciation of this savage country is obtained from the crags of A' Mhaighdean.

I was uneasy about the appearance of the west. Great black clouds were piling up and racing inland. Already Beinn Airidh Charr was enveloped and the dull clarity of impending storm was on everything. I kept climbing. Then came a clap of wind like thunder as air and rock collided. The wind cracked across the mountain and down came the rain in a hissing torrent. The clouds pressed down over me. No use going back as I was already soaked, so I kept on, clinging hard to avoid becoming part of the wind.

On tops there were some pinnacles to get over and it was an anxious moment for me until they were negotiated. Up here the wind was a scream, the pinnacles acting as a sounding instrument. I crawled the last few yards to the cairn to avoid the rain, converted now into ice particles that hit like grit.

To get back meant turning into the storm. The south face was a steep rock wall and unsheltered. The only thing for it was to descend, if possible on the north side, away from the tent, and traverse back to it round the mountain. An open gully of steep snow looked promising. I dared not glissade it, not knowing what lay below. It was a wonderful moment when I stepped out

of the wind into its shelter. There were no obstacles and the
gully led me down to a lochan from which sheets of water were
being torn. Its outlet was by a high waterfall but that day the
water was being blown straight into the air. Down by its course
I went and was soon at the point where I had started.

By now the water was running out of me. Eagerly I anticipated a change of clothing and a meal. I would soon be at my
tent. My landmark was an overhanging crag, but I could see no
sign of the tent. Then I saw the green spot, and on it an over-
turned stove, cooking pans, and a few scraps of rain-sodden food.
Of my tent, sleeping-bag, groundsheet, and spare clothing there
was no sign. I cursed myself for taking my rucksack to the hill
and not leaving it behind fully packed to protect my stuff. What
was I to do now? It was late and darkness was falling.

Now, unsuspected by me until I came to the head of Fionn
Loch, there is a house in this No Man's Land. A house, more-
over, from which I saw smoke coming, before the mist closed on
A' Mhaighdean. I had just time to get to it before dark if I
hurried. Feeling rather like a tramp asking for shelter, I
knocked at the door praying that the family would not be abed.
It was opened readily and I was invited in before I had even said
a word. True hospitality!

In a moment I had towels and an assortment of clothing to put
on. And then came an omelet, the king of omelets, that even
now, as I write, fills me with reverence. Warm and happy, I
was glad when the family filed in to pay me homage, Mr.
MacRae, Mrs. MacRae, and the two six-foot sons, Andy and
Callum. In this wild spot, especially so early in the year, I could
see I was quite an event. Soon I was telling them stories of life
in Glasgow, my work, political views, etc., and everything was
eagerly lapped up. We had some grand laughs for this was a
family full of fun, and it was late when we retired.

It was still wild on the following morning but in such good
company I was not a bit worried. Andy kept popping in and out
of the room so much I wondered what he was doing. It was
explained when in trooped the two girls, released from school for
half an hour. Andy was the teacher—on the strength of a
school-leaving certificate—and school was just another room in
the house. For teaching his sisters the county were paying him
a humble sum. Verily, necessity forces strange arrangement.

That afternoon saw us all out hunting for my missing property. There is nothing like local knowledge, for Mr. MacRae went straight to the tent wedged in some rocks, and in the same uncanny way took me to where my sleeping-bag lay in a burn blown up with water as if it enshrouded a body. That afternoon the whole glen was roaring with falling water tuned to different pitches by the wind.

It takes a lot of courage to live in a place like that. The MacRaes get food in bulk every six months, rowing it up the whole length of Fionn Loch by boat. For bread and papers it it necessary to cross over the shoulder of Beinn Làir down to Maree-side. Living out of the world like this, one would imagine that they would get on each other's nerves. Far from that being the case, there was a unity and happiness in the family that I have never met elsewhere. "If one of them gets anything the others must share it," Mrs. MacRae told me. If only life were like that. Nor did I need to be very witty to provoke a laugh, for laughter was never very far from them.

Tuesday came wet and wild with snow on the tops. "Leave it till to-morrow," said the MacRaes. Well, I was enjoying myself, and anyhow I had not given a definite time for going back to Poolewe, so I decided on another night. All too quickly it went and on Wednesday morning, in spasmodic sunshine, I said goodbye to my very good friends.

It was evening when I got to Poolewe, just in time to stop a search-party. Alarmed at my non-appearance, the postman had sent round the fiery cross, thinking the worst. I was mildly rebuked but given a great welcome and I have happy memories of that evening.

Weather wet and wild decided me on flying to the Cairngorms where I found the sun, and it was two years later in another May before I came back to fulfil my plan. This time I came by Loch Maree and across the high pass to Fionn Loch. Never will I forget the first sight of the glen as it was that evening, rich with a sunflood of colour. The loch mirrored the blue of the sky and the peaks were brittle with rock and shadows. On top of the pass in the green moss of a little waterfall, purple saxifrage was blooming. Lower down the shrill pipe of a greenshank was magic music.

The people were not expecting me. I saw Andy at the door

but he quickly disappeared to be followed by his father. "By God, it's Tommy," he shouted as he came out. It was a grand reunion. That night we had a *céilidh* with the family singing and the melodeon going. I was led to the nest of a twite too, the first I had ever seen.

With the warning "And be sure to keep off those dirty black rocks", ringing in my ears, I set off in sunshine for Mullach Coire Mhic Fhearchair. A steep wild little glen with great crags enclosing was the introduction. As I gained height Loch Ewe appeared beyond Beinn Airidh Charr. Meadow pipits were everywhere singing to earth in exultant dives, wings thrown back and tails elevated. Wheatears "chacked" from the boulders and once I surprised a ring ouzel in song. The "kek-kek-kek" of a peregrine falcon was a sound I did not anticipate. In an instant I had the bird in the glasses as it swept across a cliff face in a blue flash of speed. I was to see a lot of that wonderful flier before I left.

My peak had a delightful ridge on it, and with splendid views on either side, I crossed over to Sgùrr Ban. Cloud shadows raced over the Strath na Shellag and beyond a peak of beautiful shape I could see the Summer Isles. An Teallach and my old friends the Fannichs were at hand, recalling joyful days among the snow. South of where Loch Maree was hidden were the grey peaks of Torridon. The song of a snow-bunting was a delightful surprise here. In vain I looked for its nest.

Strolling back to the house that night from Strath na Shellag I felt that this was the peak of living. My spirits were as high as the eagle I could see soaring over the top of A' Mhaighdean. Nor will I forget the chicken soup and chicken that the kindly Mrs. MacRae had ready for me.

The days that followed were equally good. I had the rare privilege of watching the courtship of the black-throated diver. There were three of them and a complicated affair it was with much billing and touching of breasts. Surely this is one of the most beautiful of all water-birds. In bed I could listen to the snipe drumming, the sharp pipe of oyster-catcher, the hurried notes of sandpiper, mingling voices of curlew, red-shank and greenshank. This is the dawn chorus of this wild country.

At last it was time to go. I had a rendezvous with Matt in

Sutherland and it was my intention to walk by hill paths to Inchnadamph.

The whole family came with me to the path to see me off. The first time, Mr. MacRae told me, that he had ever come to see any one off. I felt duly honoured. It was a sad good-bye to people I had come to regard as more than friends. Andy and Callum came with me to the summit of the first pass where they were going to do some draining. Andy carried my pack. It was raining and the peaks were in the clouds. "A dirty day for working," said Andy as he handed me my pack. We shook hands. I felt very lonely as I walked away into the hills.

12

Sutherland

RAIN was falling and the lifeless countryside drooped under low, creeping mists. My impressions were confirmed. I was a fool to come to this bleak country of Sutherland. From the peaks of Ross I had been repelled by its bare moorlands and gaunt peaks. Repelled but fascinated too by the legend of its remoteness, and now, here I was tramping up towards the village of Elphin. "A dirty night," I called to a white-bearded old man at his cottage door. His "Och yes, a fine night for the grasses", was a surprising reply. Head down I walked on, wishing I were one of the grasses. Never had I seen a more unprepossessing land.

My arrangement was to meet Matt that night in Inchnadamph so I strode on imagining all sorts of reasons to prevent his being there. Imperceptibly my surroundings became more verdant. Moorland gave way to green grass and birch trees grew in the gullies. Along a line of steep crags on my right a peregrine falcon flew. Ahead was Loch Assynt. I was as good as there and beautiful turf invited camping. All I wanted now was my friend Matt. And just half an hour later he turned up, starving with hunger after a twenty-hour journey. So we pitched the tents, got the stove purring, had a meal, and turned into our sleeping-bags. Even the rain had a pleasant sound.

Rain and mist covered everything on the following morning, but we set off for Ben More Assynt to "break the stillness that ordinarily rests on this remote region". An eagle carrying a lapwing in its talons was an interesting sight, but all too soon the mist enveloped us and there was nothing to do but plod upwards. In no time it seemed we were on the summit. The only snag was that under our feet was grass, and not the sparkling white Cambrian quartzite for which this peak is famous.

An examination of the map did not help, and just as we were getting completely bewildered, a hole appeared in the mist. Opposite us a vast hill-side was opening up. Wind slashed the

77

clouds, and suddenly a peak of glistening white was thrown against blue sky. There could be no mistaking it. Quickly I took a bearing to it, plotted in a back ray and found we were on Breabag, an outlying spur of Conamheall. Thereafter, it was just a case of climbing over that peak and following the ridge on to Sutherland's greatest peak. But what a crossing that was!

The wind that swept the tops clear was gathering up the clouds and rushing them in wads of cumulus through the glens at our feet. To be above such scudding clouds gave a feeling of being airborne, cruising the skies on a mountain top. All the peaks, An Teallach, Ben Hope, Loyal, Canisp, Suilven, etc. were sticking above this racing cloud-sea which extended in all directions except to the north-east. Visibility was needle sharp and the feast of colours—blues, browns, and greys—was amazing. Even the Cairngorms were visible, a great lump cut in the centre by the cleft of the Lairig Ghrù. An intense heat from a cloudless sky followed, clearing away the low clouds, bringing us down to earth again. Reluctantly we left the tops for descent to camp. Where did I get my impression that this was a bleak land, I wondered.

The sun shining woke us up next morning. Birds were singing, and over Quinag a great cloud was breaking. "That is our peak," said Matt. And from its top we had a view unsurpassed in my memory. Across Loch Assynt, above a moorland dotted with little lochans, lay Suilven, its huge rounded boss towering above the low moors. West and south-west the eye ranged over the Torridon mountains to the peaks of Skye, and up past the hills of Harris to the Butt of Lewis. The sandy bays fringing the coast and hundreds of lochans dotted everywhere, with the Atlantic beyond, made a unique and fascinating prospect, the predominating colour of which was sky reflected blue. Even the distant rocky pancake of North Rona was visible—the isolated little island where Dr. Fraser Darling studied the seals.

From the cairn we descended for a rock-climb and got a sparkling three hundred feet on steep sound rock. Continuing over the tops made a grand ridge-walk, but it was the north peak that gave the most spectacular views. We were looking down on the meeting-place of the three lochs, Carn Bawn, Glendhu, and Gleneonl. Across the coast was the bird island of Handa.

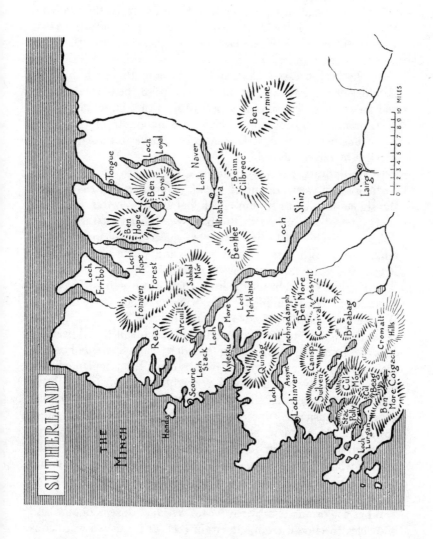

SUTHERLAND

THE MINCH

That day the sun shone its full round and back in camp we found our skins suffering for it.

The following day, we vowed, was to be a rest day but Canisp invited, and once on its top we just could not resist the challenge of Suilven—the Pillar Fell—with its rock fangs sticking above a lonely little loch. Heat haze marred the view, but the ridge traverse over Caisteal Liath—the Grey Castle—to Meall Beag was delightful, if easy. Coming back to camp that night over the shoulder of Canisp, the grey sides and tops of the quartzite peaks had an afterglow of sunset as beautiful as that on winter snows. A surprising thing to us on Suilven was its wealth of vegetation, ferns, heather, wood sorrel, primroses, violets, roseroot, etc., all striving to reach the top.

Next morning we had a shock. There was no mail-car to Ledmore and we were out of bread. However, fate saved us in the shape of a lift to Elphin and a loaf from a crofter. So, with energy saved and a loaf in the bag, we "horsed" it through the hills to a birch-clad lochan near that queer-named loch, Skinaskink. And with sixty-pound packs and a trackless boulder-strewn waste to cross, it was "horsing".

Our camp was a beautiful little spot, green and turfy, where a mountain burn tumbled on to fringing sands of the lochan. We were in a hollow between Cùl Mór and Cùl Beag, a spot isolated enough to satisfy even my rebel spirit. Wheatears chacked from the surrounding boulders, sandpipers bobbed at the water's edge, and from the woods came the familiar trills of silvery-voiced wrens and willow-warblers. Redshanks flitted and always there was the shrilling music of these truly great mountain musicians, the curlews. In the mosses too, were flowers of the sundew, sorrel, alpine ladies' mantle, and violet. Through the birch grove, An Stac—usually called Stac Polly despite what the map says—appeared as a double top, steep and inviting. So instead of resting after our bag-carrying labours, we set off at five p.m. for its top.

What a glorious climb that was! We had dozens of ribs and pinnacles to choose from, all virgin rock as far as we were concerned. We chose a great eight-hundred-foot rib of pink rock terminating in a sharp point that jutted out colourfully against the blue sky. Matt made a splendid lead and although in rubbers, I found the rock-climbing standard severe throughout. The last pitch on to the spire was the height of rock-climbing enjoyment. No eagle ever had a better perch. Professor Heddle has described its pinnacled ridge as being like "a porcupine in a state of extreme irascibility". And that adequately describes it. The scramble along the porcupine's back must be one of the finest little ridge scrambles in all Scotland.

I could well believe the statement that this western coastline with its many indentations and sea lochs reminds one of the finest scenery in Norway. Against the dark curves of bays and islands the Atlantic glittered silver with sunset. All the tops were flushed beautiful tints and in the depths of the shadowy glens the lochans were splashes of mercury. It was eleven p.m. when we got to camp that night, having been on the march for sixteen hours.

Now I have to record a crime! Sunrise was perfect but the flawless horizon was marred by only one cloud. Our food was finished. Despite careful rationing all that remained in our larder was a little scrap of hard bread, a scrape of butter, and a little tea. But Matt has always something in that rucksack of his, and from its depths he produced a length of fishing-line and a hook. A search beneath a boulder and we had a worm. Into the loch we tossed our weighted bait. . . .

Hopefully we started up Cùl Mór, the great back, first of all by an abortive rock-climb which we had to descend completely for there was no escape. A rock-climb did take us to the top but the rock was rotten and quite unsuited to difficult climbing.

Views of the Fannich mountains were particularly good but our tummies drove us down to inspect our fishing-line. Fearfully we hauled it in. A flash of silver and we howled a hurrah. Saved by a trout! We melted our butter and had a fry of its delicious pink meat. And there was still enough left over for yet another meal.

Thus refreshed, and since it was still early in the day, we started up the little back, Cùl Beag. From its top we looked to a new An Stac, a craggy point sticking above a sparkling lochan. It was a still night and back in camp the midges—I had forgotten what they were like—made us glad to retire to our flea-bags. Our hopes of a breakfast were dashed too, for our fishing-line broke as we hauled it in. Of course there was a big fish on it!

What a torturing night followed! Midges and sunburn gave

us no rest, and packing up was made more than aggravating by
the attentions of the former. The glorious sunrise and charm of
our situation went unheeded. Our retreat became a rout. We
were hungry and in silence tramped across the hills to Loch
Lurgain which was on a mail-car route.

Our luck was in. The mail-car—one per day—rattled up as
we touched down on the road and bore us to Ullapool. Just a
few minutes later and we would have been well and truly sunk.

I forget all the good things we bought in that shop. What I
do remember is returning to a lovely little bay at Ardmair and
settling down to the meal of a lifetime prepared by the worthy
Matt. Our camp was a cheery spot, a place of nesting terns,
redshank, oyster-catchers and sandpipers. Mergansers, eider
ducks, red-throated divers, and surprisingly, a great crested
grebe, provided interest without stirring from the shade of the
tent door.

All we had time for in the short while remaining was a traverse
of Ben More Cóigeach, up by the "Rock" and back over the long
summit ridge. We were over the border into Ross proper, and
despite the blazing sun, Sutherland and its mountains appeared
a forbidding land, frigid and austere. Never was there a greater
contradiction.

13

Farthest North

"The third of June and look at it," I moaned. Rain battered the train windows, washing them as though by water thrown in bucketfuls. There was nothing to see: all the clouds in the world seemed to be massed on the Cairngorms. And this was my embarkation leave and I was bound for the wilds of Sutherland with food for a week in my rucksack and no tent. I had fooled myself into thinking that in June a sleeping-bag, stove, and food was all that was necessary.

What of my fine plans if the weather were like this for a week or more? I had worked out a route across Scotland's most northern mountainland and it was beginning to look as if it would be a rout and not a route. For this northland does not offer tourist accommodation, in fact it shuns it, and such inns as were once convenient to climbers have been closed for many years. It is an old Highland story—like the clearances—and is almost as effective in keeping the land for the few.

At Carr Bridge my sorry ruminations were disturbed as a new traveller got in. Even for war-time his dress was bizarre—from his wrinkled red tartan tie to his much patched rubber boots. His trousers were thin hosepipes of grey extending to a brown tweed waistcoat, partly covered by a navy blue serge jacket. A grey moustache, yellowed teeth, and the communicative manner of the very old gave a clue to his age.

Within two minutes he told us that he was going to try to get his wife out of Inverness Infirmary where she had been for five weeks. He had the soft speech of the west and I was not surprised to hear that he came from North Uist.

"The Lord will help me this day for He knows I am on His side."

Perhaps he divined my surprise at this rather unexpected remark for he looked at me intently and added with some heat:

"Yes, I know the Book from Genesis to Jeremiah and the Lord

is revealing it to me more and more every time I read." He
waited for me to say something but I had nothing to say.

"Yes, I know the Bible better than all your scholars, lawyers,
and doctors. God is in me here." He pointed to his heart. "I
don't want learning." Up went his hand in a dramatic gesture.
"May the Lord give me understanding, understanding and the
knowledge to do right."

He pointed at me.

"Where is your learning to-day? See what it has brought
you. It is the devil's work and Armageddon is at hand. I know
it. I know it. For the Lord has revealed it to me."

The accusation in his eye and certainty in his manner were
rather startling. Then in a quieter voice he told us his history.

"Nine and a half years in the army. I was eleven and a half
stones in those days and as strong as a bull. Yes, and the finest
sportsman in the army, not in the regiment, but in the whole
army. Every prize I took. Yes, and even yet I'll outfight, out-
run, outswim, or outdrink any man of my age."

He struck an attitude with his fists clenched in the manner of
a boxer and gave us a pantomime of all the jaws he had broken
and a recital of his talents; of how when all his money had been
spent on drink he had walked in the dead of winter all the way
from London to Inverness.

"I can make a pair of trousers and vest as good as any tailor.
But not the jacket. I was never taught the jacket. I'm knacky
with my hands, knacky. Yes, I can do any job at all, any mortal
job, working a croft, carpentering or building."

His financial position quite distressed me. Twenty-seven and
sixpence was the total income of the two of them, his wife and
himself. There was no bus from the cottage and he had to walk
the seven miles each way. "Yes, even in the snow," to draw his
pension and carry the groceries home on his back.

He had an idea of getting some timber and building a cottage
near Inverness. "I will look for a place when I am in Inverness
for I have the timber for the asking." He had no doubts about
his ability, a frail old man, lost without his wife but full of zeal
as to the future, Armageddon or no Armageddon.

The troubles of a fellow-man having put my minor misfortunes
in true perspective, I looked at the rain with a less jaundiced eye
and by the time Lairg was reached had even contrived a kind of

hilarity, a hilarity which was severely jolted when I was told that
there was no mail-car to Durness for another six hours. Luckily
they have a café at Lairg so I passed the time by drinking tea.

Sitting in the train from Glasgow to Lairg had made me stiff,
so at midday I ventured out. The rain was only a drizzle now,
and encouraged by a brightness, I went up to a wooded slope,
a place of birdsong and flitting bullfinches and redpolls. The
rain had stopped and the clouds were lifting from the hills.
Unmistakably a change was brewing, for a keen east wind
had risen.

By two p.m. the sun was shining and the mists of morning
were floating as beautiful cumuli, dappling the blue hills with
racing shadows. Lairg, by its verdant green and fine woods at
the edge of Loch Shin, came as a surprise, for on the map it
looks a bleak place on the edge of a peaty nothing.

Impatiently I waited for the mail-car, full of the expectation
that this strange land of Sutherland arouses. At last the mails
were loaded, passengers aboard—a full complement of two, including myself—and we rattled away towards one of my life-
long ambitions.

All this land was new to me and my heart rejoiced to recognize
Beinn Klibreck and see Ben Loyal leap from the moor in rocky
spires. The vastness of those moors made a profound impression
on me. This afternoon they were warm-coloured by the sun and
threaded by blue streams and dotted with little gems of lochs.
But all too vividly I could picture them as they must have been
half a dozen hours before, sullen and waterlogged, beaten by
wind and rain.

Altnaharrie, a long climb up to a high point on the road, and
I recognized Loch Coulside. Ahead was a tiny house marked on
the map "Inchkinloch". This I had chosen as my jumping-off
spot. I paid my dues and slung on my heavy sack. My way lay
over the shoulder of Ben Loyal, by what I anticipated would
be bad bogland, to a little loch set in the heart of the mountains.
This loch had a peculiar hold on my imagination—for no reason
at all except its setting. I made my way towards it invigorated
by the joy of being at last in this great country.

What an evening that was! An evening of blue-washed hills
and bluer lochs, lochs the colour of blue dye that had seeped
into the very burns. For contrast there was the near mass of

Klibreck, a great sweep of russet patched with shadow. Shadows in Sutherland, this bare land, assume the significance of physical features, like the vasty sky that domes this edge of Scotland where it fringes the northern sea.

My prediction as to the wetness of the ground proved accurate, for above Loch Coulside by the saturated ground which is Loch Haluim, I found a morass which was barely passable. But for compensation there was the beauty of waving bog-cotton and the peak of Loyal, an upstanding rock pinnacle towards which a birch gully twisted. My watch said seven p.m., so parking my bag, I followed up that gully by birch greens to rock. The sun had been behind clouds but broke through as I popped my head over the top.

Below me was the Kyle of Tongue, its yellow sands and green woods floodlit against the vivid sea. Beyond Loch Erribol was a rocky Ailsa Craig shape. From it, reaching back in waves of increasing bulk inland, were shaggy rollers of mountains, blue-black against the sun. Ben Hope, my legendary peak, was opposite, supported on three rocky pillars clung with birches. Above a little loch at my feet was a sensational crag rising to another of Loyal's peaks. A finer panorama of ocean has never been mine. All that was missing was the Orkney Islands.

Happy now, I got back to my bag and pushed on by another loch and a burn that cascaded amongst birches and willows. Teal and mallard were nesting up here, and lower down were ring ouzels. Then my loch hove in sight, straight below me and fringed by an oasis of green amongst golden whins. Steep crags rose from its eastern shore, and from the piled boulders twisted birch grew. West was the bold front of Ben Hope. Perched on the shore was a house.

How I wished Matt had been with me! Often he told me that in his P.O.W. camp he had pictured the little loch with its birches and sandy shore by Cùl Beag where we had caught the fish. Here was his dream come true: a sandy shore, steep crags hung with birches, and high hills for company.

Over Ben Hope the sun was setting in streamers of gold that filtered the purple of its shadowed face. The loch, still as a mirror, held all the yellows and reds of the sunset sky. Around me, snipe were at their nesting note, a sound I always associate with great days on the hills. Sandpipers were calling and flitting over the water. A twite was singing its linnet-like little song as I turned into my bag at midnight.

The song of a willow-warbler, repeated time after time and note for note, was my coming to consciousness. It was ten a.m. before I got up, nor was I ashamed, for I needed the sleep. Breakfast and a sandwich and I was off for Ben Hope. Rain was sweeping the hills but the air was mild and blinks of sun gave encouragement.

I traversed the peak from the south, and all the time I felt I was racing the bad weather, for thunder was sounding in the west, and creeping inward were huge black clouds below which the peaks of the Beinn Hee group were wan. However, I won the race by about a minute, just in time to get shelter. Over the Kyle it was sunny, the moorlands glittering with peat-hags. To-day the tide was out and long sands reached out to sea.

It is a fascinating place to be, this high peak above the north tip of Scotland. Loch Hope, black as ink, was three thousand feet below me, and over a peaty tongue of land was Loch Eriboll. Foinnebheinn and its rain-blurred neighbours looked tremendous, rising in rock to shapely peaks linked by inviting ridges. My only company was a ring ouzel that sang its staccato phrases to cheer me.

Down over rock debris and other signs of glaciation I came to the floor of the upper corrie, a place of little lochans and strewn boulders. The bad weather cleared away and I sat warm in the sun watching a greenshank and some sandpipers at the water's edge. I thought of climbing Ben Loyal for the sunset and waiting for the sunrise but on the way down it started to thunder and before long a downpour had blotted out everything.

I mentioned a house earlier on in this story: this was uninhabited but securely locked up. In view of my bedraggled condition and the need for shelter I decided it was justifiable to force an entry. This was accomplished, after searching for the key under all the local boulders and in the niche above the door, by forcing myself through a tiny window high up, whose latch yielded to the deft twist of a pocket-knife. Inside were a couple of couches, a bed, table and chairs. Obviously the place was in use, probably during the lambing season and sheep gathering. A good fire going and a meal on the hob made it seem a cosy spot indeed. By candlelight I read, with the flickering fire for company, F. B.

Young's epic poem, *The Island*. I would not have changed my "digs" for the most palatial hotel in Britain.

The sound of rain thrown on the window by wind buffets awoke me in the morning. The hills were dimmed by fierce squalls but clear of mist and I felt optimistic as to the future. By the time I had eaten a leisurely breakfast, juggling with dried eggs and the synthetic stuffs a war forces on a camper, the sun was beginning to break through. A traverse of Ben Loyal was indicated and the obstacle of the burn being negotiated by a tight-rope act on twin strands of loose wire, the hill was all mine.

I went by the east shore of the loch, Loch an Dithreibh by name, in and out amongst boulders torn from the steep crags above and supporting, somehow, a forest of silver birch and mountain ash. It was more like an April morning the way the sun played hide-and-seek with the clouds. I hoped to see a peregrine falcon, for it was a likely place, but I was unlucky. Bird song was fine, however, and from the loch came the weird sound of loons, black-throated divers.

Leaving the loch, I now skirted north-east, heading for the most seaward peak of Sgorr Chaonsaid, so as to traverse the mountain from north to south. Looking back, I could see Sgorr a' Chléirich, a tooth of grey rock as sensational-looking as the third pinnacle of Sgùrr nan Gillean. The steep slope I was climbing was a colourful garden of globe-flowers, tormentil, violets, buttercups and daisies, broad-leafed willow-herb, blue-bells, spotted orchis, and even wood sanicle. Tree pipits were singing from the scattered birches and even at fifteen hundred feet I saw robins and thrushes. From under my feet a wood-cock rose, quite possibly nesting up here.

I had hoped for a rock-climb on my peak but the intense vegetation extended to the rocks. Every known lichen must have hung on the crags. Nor was my slope prepossessing. It was evident I was on bare rock covered by a skin of moss, for large areas of foothold kept slipping away. But this dangerous traverse was made worth while by the glory of cushion pinks and starry saxifrage that made a rock garden of the mossy face. Also growing was a thick-leafed little Alpine with whitish-pink flowers.

My route landed me on the very summit and what I sought was there, the Orkneys, rising in three hog-backs out of the sea sixty degrees true north of my position. The whole landscape had that hard, clean look peculiar to showery weather. The tiny houses, dots of white on the edge of the Kyle, were most attractive to see. Ben Hope I was interested to note has almost a replica of its shape in the protruding buttresses that front it as Meallan Liath, Creag Riabhach Mhór, and Creag Riabhach Beag; which would seem to indicate to a non-geologist a hard core of matter that is undergoing parallel weathering. Perhaps the rounder form of Ben Hope was once like these craggy peaks which front it.

Heavy showers were piling over the peaks of Beinn Hee to the south-west, in contrast to the serene skies over Loyal and the blue hills to the east. Quickly I made over to my next top and got there just in time to shelter. There was a darkness on the peak and sleet came slashing across on the edge of a sudden squall of wind. In the lulls that came as quickly as the storms, I managed the various tops.

I must confess to a disappointment with Ben Loyal, for it shows great promise of climbs but fulfils none. The rock is a kind of granite totally unsuited for rock-climbing but spectacular in form. That day of storm showed it off to advantage as the mist played amongst its pinnacles.

Once off the top I was in sunshine and out of the wind. Buck-bean growing out of the water of a peat-hag on the moor was a pretty sight and I cursed the lack of film that prevented photography. What opportunities I lost during that day of storm and sunshine! I got to the house as the rain settled in the glen for the evening.

All night it poured, but by the time I had packed my gear in the morning it had cleared to showers. Now I wanted to get to Loch Stack-side, and if you look at the map you will see that it is quite a long way off. Nor is there a track until you get to Strath More. I decided to go by the Allt an Achaidh Mhóir. My pack was lighter by a few items of food so I fooled myself there was little weight in it and swung off.

The going was rough but the foaming burn (*allt* means a burn) made for a certain amount of interest. Bens Hope and Loyal were in mist. Sooner than I thought I was on top of the pass and traversing west towards the Strath. Here the sun broke through, making silver of the wet rock-slabs on Beinn Hee. From below me a cock merlin rose out of the heather, its pointed wings and slate colour showing perfectly.

Strath More was an inviting place to descend to with its wide river reaching up to a most imposing aspect of Ben Hope. Straight ahead of me to the west my pass climbed to a tiny gap high in the ridge. I had a light meal and pushed on by a fine track into a region of wild rocky corries overhung with the inevitable birch. Showers were more frequent now but it was not until I topped the col and saw a mighty rain-blurred cone, Ben Stack, that I realized I was in for trouble. Cold and stinging, the huge veil whipped across, right in my face. I crouched under my oilskin but there was no sign of a lull so I went on as fast as I could, to keep warm.

Suddenly I came to a wonderful place. Through a curtain of rain, beyond an inky loch and in the space between the dim crag of Arkle and the shadowy cone of Ben Stac was a weird jumble of flat-topped mounds, blurred and mysterious, cradling below their bulging shoulders lochans, gleams of water that might have been the abiding place of everything supernatural. The whole gaunt and naked landscape was empty of man or any sign of man, a place where the elements could roar and thrash their rains on the tumbled glacier beds belonging to past geological time. All was blotted out in a tremendous rainstorm.

I was grateful for the first sign of civilization, a house marked on the map "Lone". Unfortunately it was empty and disused but on the map only one and a half miles away was another house marked "Airdchuillin". I was wet and not too well off for food, so I decided to go to it and ask for lodging.

The house proved to be rather more pretentious than the usual run of keepers' places and in some trepidation I knocked at the door, fully conscious of my tramp-like condition. But here was true Highland hospitality. "You'd better come in," were the kind-faced man's first words. A room was placed at my disposal immediately and a tea of home-made scones and bannocks was ready by the time I had changed my clothes. Mr. Scobbie presided in the absence of his wife but if it was an inconvenience he showed no sign of it. The same hearty welcome was extended to me by Mrs. Scobbie when she came in and I was treated as if I were an old friend of the family. To come to a house like this after a spell of lonely sojourning is like coming home.

A stormy sunset had us all shaking our heads as to the weather prospects.

But we were wrong. Morning came with all the glory of early June at its finest. Arkle was my peak. Arkle and its neighbours which had captured my fancy when I had seen their quartz peaks from the top of Quinag. Now I could get to grips with them. Many rock buttresses invited on Arkle but I had a long day planned and I was anxious to get on to the tops for the uninterrupted views north and west which I knew the peak must give.

In the vital air and sunshine of that perfect morning, every upward step was a lifting of the heart. I had been looking forward to seeing all my old friends, Quinag, Ben More, Suilven, etc., but even my imagination was outstripped as they rose in purple-blue bunched huge over the low moors. How good it was to see them: the unmistakable rock pillars of Suilven; the point of Stac Polly, Cùl Mór and Canisp; and west of them the old boys, Ben More and Conamheall. A fainter blue and appearing over the arm of Breabàg were the Loch Droma peaks of Ben Dearg and Conaa Mheall showing as two cones connected by a high shoulder. Left of Stac Polly it gladdened me to identify the edge of An Teallach.

Such a pre-view spurred me on to the summit, a narrow edge of splintered quartzite almost as dazzling to the eye as snow. Around were the most contrasting colours I have ever seen, snow-like mountains, Mediterranean seas, the green islands of Badcall Bay, and the moorland heaths to Cape Wrath alive with lochans and silvery streams.

I had no realization my peaks were so bare of vegetation. The whole chain of Foinnebheinn I could see was composed entirely of quartz blocks strewn to glen level. Down to Loch an Easain Uane I struck, by the roughest hill-side I have ever been on. Every footstep had to be picked with care, and I was glad to take to some delightfully sound rock as a relief. In the hollow between Foinnebheinn and Arkle I ate with relish some oatcake and an egg, savouring the situation as much as the repast.

Up by Coire a Chouiteir, over a little pinnacle and another couple of tops and I was on Foinnebheinn's summit. The view over the dotted lochs and fretted coast was a replica of my memory of the view from Quinag. Mist was creeping over the tops now, and from Gaineamh Mhór and Ceann Garbh I saw nothing at all.

In this mountain fastness there is a celebrated crag by a wild loch, Creag Dionard is its name, called after the loch, Loch Dionard. It is not an easy place to get to, but I saw a way of including it on my return journey. Cnoc Duail was the way, past the Buachaille Etive Mór-like crags of A' Choir Gorm. What a feast of rock exploring is on this remote face!

I came to Loch Dìonard. Like another Sròn na Cìche the rock rises in a thousand-foot sweep. Down its huge face poured a mighty waterfall in spate with the recent rains. Examining the rock, I saw exciting problems awaiting the explorer for the place abounded in grand situations, and it appeared to me as though quite a few rock formations were in its make-up. If only Matt had been with me!

Deep heather that made hard going took me from here to where a path led to An Dubh Loch, a beautiful corrie in the mossy face of Meall Horn. I had been feeling tired climbing the sixteen hundred feet to the top of the Bealach but the view from the summit rejuvenated me. The whole of south-west Sutherland was sunlit. On the sea, silvery with sunset, the islands of Badcall Bay were ebony. Above me over the green top of Meall Horn, an eagle was performing diving acrobatics. A line of crags led to the top inviting me to get up there. My tiredness vanished and I scrambled on sound rock into the sunshine.

All the beauty of Sutherland was mine, from Ben Hope down into Ross, each peak having its natural colour undimmed by shadows or tinged with blue. An Teallach was sharp and hard now. The Orkneys had crept out of the sea, and west, on the Atlantic silver, was the long line of the Outer Isles.

It was eleven p.m. when I got back to the house but there was no complaint about my late hours or the fact that my dinner had been kept waiting. Fresh trout and potatoes, custard and jelly, and lashings of tea was a fit finish to a memorable day. Bath and bed, and I was ready for both.

I was awakened by Mr. Scobbie with the news that a pair of black-throated divers were below my window. Imagine watching a pair of black-throated divers from your bedroom window! Every marking of their velvety plumage was visible. How beautifully the black throat is drawn on delicate grey.

Unfortunately the rain came, and after a visit to a hoodie's nest the weather became impossible. Still we had a good day at "the conversation", exchanging yarns and ideas. Mr. Scobbie's son, Bill, was a keen bird-man so we had plenty to say to each other. I felt I had earned a day off anyhow, so my inactivity did not come amiss.

But I was disappointed when the next morning brought more rain and dense clouds pressing down from the north. It seemed a hopeless sort of a day but to my delight it cleared to a breezy day of showers and sun. Round Loch Stack on the hunt for red-throated divers I went by a morass of bog, but all I saw was an excited greenshank. Ben Stack was the natural way to finish and up its steep birch-slopes and rocky ribs I went to the narrow summit ridge to arrive there in sunshine.

Most fascinating to me in the varied view from the summit was the lane of rocky mounds stretching from the mountains to the sea. No doubt that it was worn by ice for the vegetation has been scalped from the harder material leaving smooth rock slabs crowning their flattened tops. Loch Laxford and Inchard are the culminating points of the glacier system as it appeared to me, sitting on top of Ben Stack.

In the light of a marvellous sunset I came down. A fine evening in the Highlands is in my opinion the greatest manifestation of nature. That was an evening as fine as any I have ever seen. The whole glen was afire, each tree and blade of grass glowing as though lit from within.

The man who said it could be winter any day of the year on the Scottish hills certainly knew his Highlands. Morning brought a howling west wind and a downpour from swirling grey clouds that opened and closed on Arkle. From my window I could see a waterfall high on the mountain smoking like a chimney-stack as the water went up instead of down.

Bill ferried me across the stormy loch which was the journey's end of my leave. He could have let me walk the one and a half miles to the road-end to meet the mail-car and thus avoid a wetting, but that was not the way of the Scobbies. Climbing means more than just mountains when you meet such people.

14

The Cairngorms

THE fateful calling-up papers had arrived and I calculated that, if the firm let me leave on Saturday, I should have just four days of freedom before being engulfed in the army. Four days! It was May and I pictured sunshine in the glens, cloud shadows racing over the dappled peaks, and the sparkle of hill burns as they ran free between birches shimmering in new green. I would go to the hills and forget the war in the short glory of peace.

Where should I go? Of all the Ordnance Maps I know there is none so compelling as the *Cairngorms*. Contours steep and brown enclose single dotted lines—tracks—that climb over and round them, by blue lochs and rivers and green stretching woods of pine, free from civilizing roads. And the names of Monadh Mór, MacDhui, the Pools of Dee, Braeriach, sound the final attraction. It was a tiny spot amongst the dark shading (which means wild rocky country) marked "Shelter Stone" which decided me. Here was a place I had always wanted to visit. I pictured myself basking in the sun beside the icy waters of Loch Avon over which the stone sits. It has a reputation for inaccessibility.

Four days' food, spare paraffin for the Primus stove, sleeping-bag, spare clothes, etc., made a tidy load and my overloaded Bergan, like myself, creaked a bit as I tried it on. "Good training for the army," I registered mentally. The sun was shining when I arrived in Aviemore by the Sunday paper train. Over the blueness of Rotheimurchus Forest dark clouds were piling on the hills but my heart was lighter than the rucksack and I stepped it out, impatient to get into the wilderness and among the pines.

Two miles to Coylum Bridge and a yellow finger of post pointed to "The Lairig Ghrù". A path of pine needles stretched invitingly and birds were singing in the woods. The adventure was begun and I swung on happily. What a wonder of track that is, especially where the old Caledonian pines thin out high above the river, and the little gullies of birches brilliant with green and silver are revealed in glorious contrast to the sombre tints of pine and hill. Here, a hen goosander circled round me calling harshly. Big clouds kept piling over the peaks but did not obscure the sun for long.

High up, below Sròn na Lairig, a peat-bog with bleaching arms of bog pine invited a fire. It is good material for burning and in a few moments I had a can of tea boiling above its blue flame. Below me was the sunlit forest straggling upward to Carn Elrig. The summit of the pass felt obligingly near. A dipper flashed past and from the burn-side a thin burst of song finishing in a trill of elation told of a wren.

Soon I was amongst the boulders and, taking it slowly, breasted the rise to the summit of the pass with an ease which surprised me and my forty-pound pack. Soft sunshine lit the sloping screes to beautiful tints of red. Beyond my wilderness of scarred hill-side, the verdant country of Speyside was far below and remote as another world.

The climb with my heavy bag up on to the plateau by the March Burn which I had been dreading proved nothing like so desperate as I had imagined. Views across to the Angel's Peak were spectacular. Snowy corries, rich cloud patterns caressing flaring red screes, the abyss of shadow to the Lairig, made up a tremendous effect of mountain wildness appropriate to my immediate surroundings. Here on the plateau, the feeling of loneliness is emphasized by immensity of bareness—a flat expanse of grey stone breaking out of vast snowfields. I went over it, the Féith Bhuidhe, as it is called. The mournful voices of golden plover and ptarmigan were in harmony with their surroundings. To me it was music.

Suddenly the plateau edged to a steep wall of rock and frozen snow down which I had to find a way. The thrust of the great buttress of the Shelter Stone Crag plunging to Loch Avon, bathed in its upper part by the rosy tint of the low sun was magnificent beyond words. I regretted not bringing an ice-axe, but clinging to rocks which had been bared by the sun, I picked a line down. There is an insecurity about rock-climbing with a heavy pack. Lower down, beside a great waterslide, I spied through the glass and soon picked out the "Stone" from the assorted boulders piled below the crag. Some kind person had built a cairn of stones on its top. Fortunately it was not misty, otherwise it would have been difficult to find the Stone.

It was a beautiful evening and I felt at peace with the world as I tossed my bag off at the Stone's tiny entrance. Inside was a dark roomy chamber floored with thick heather, the roof being a huge boulder resting on a nest of smaller ones. The sun was on the flat slab outside and there I got the stove going to fry some bacon and black pudding. It was grand sitting there. Loch Avon had only the faintest of ripples. The rushing of burns emptying themselves from their rock-courses into the loch and their echoing murmur from the corries were the only sounds. At ten p.m. I retired to the dark hole known as the "Shelter Stone" and read by candlelight, comfortably warm in my eiderdown flea-bag.

White clouds scudding over the pinnacle of the Shelter Stone Crag, revealing it at one moment against a background of palest blue, at the next red against a gathering of dazzling cumulus, were a perfect greeting to the day. A steep snow gully cleft its left side, and fortified by a good breakfast I decided to try to climb it. Without an axe it was a stupid choice, particularly as at close quarters it proved to be much steeper than it looked.

For some three hundred feet I kicked steps which diminished in size until all I could manage, despite many blows with the iron shod toe of my boot, was the tiniest scrape. A slip off such a step was not to be thought of for there was much steep rock below, and all too well I know the speed at which an unchecked body can slither down steep frozen snow. There was another factor too: barring my way was a huge mass of loose rock balanced above me and poised on the snow ready to slide. It must have been a recent fall, I deduced, for brown stains marked the snow. That decided me. Balancing carefully on my tiny scrapes I made a cautious descent and by various little scrambles on sound rock reached the little loch below Loch Etchachan. Mist was forming on the hills and already my tops were enveloped.

By compass I did the round of the Loch Etchachan peaks finishing up on Beinn Mheadhoin. Here I waited for a clearing and was lucky. A brightness lit the mist and suddenly a great hole was torn open, revealing smoking corries hung with crags down which waterfalls tumbled. The feeling of depth below me increased as the gap widened. A flash of sunshine sparkled the wet rocks and warmed the vast brown hill-sides. That was an inspiring moment.

By the time I got back to the "Stone", it was a wonderful evening. Fish were jumping on the glass-like surface of the loch and sunshine bathed the peaks. I dined happily on my dinner-time slab and heard a twite. It was cosy that night in the "Stone", and I reflected on the luck which looks after moun-taineers, for on the way back to camp I inspected that gully again and found that the rock mass had avalanched into the corries, leaving dark scars all the way down the snow.

Another superb morning gladdened the heart as I peeped out-side the little entrance hole. It was a shame to leave the place so soon. There is a visitors' book kept here and I wondered if I would ever see the place again and deplored the folly of war when the world is such a beautiful place. My rucksack was lighter by two days' food and by the shores of Loch Avon to A'Choinneach and Bynack More I returned. Unfortunately the good weather was short-lived and the ascent of these peaks was spoiled by heavy rain. Nevertheless the sun did shine a little and its brilliance on the woods and hills was worth the rain to see such colour. I now made my way over to Rebhoan by a narrow track across a wilderness of miles of peat-hags. It was a great moment when Strathnethy lay below with its scattered pines and dense woods a haze of blue.

The bothy of Rebhoan was a delightful surprise. I expected a dilapidated, filthy old shed. Instead, I found a clean spacious room with a fire-place and rough furniture. I lost no time in getting a fire lit and was busy with a brew of tea when the door opened and a head looked in. "Excuse me, may I come in?" he asked. "Yes, do," I replied with a show of enthusiasm. Actually I resented the intrusion on my peace. But not for long. He was wearing climbing-boots and I asked him if he had been on the hill. "No, I've been bird-watching in a hide all day," he told me. "Photography?" I queried. "Merlins," he replied tersely. Soon we were exchanging experiences. He was obviously an expert naturalist and I noticed that only one of his eyes moved as he spoke. "Eric Hosking?" I asked. Yes, it was. He introduced me to his very charming wife and we had a long talk. It was a grand meeting that. He told me he had been photographing greenshank and having since seen his picture, he certainly made the most of his time.

The next day was my last and at five-thirty a.m. I said good-bye to the friendly little mice of Rebhoan which had so confidently shared my frying-pan. It was a superb morning of pale blue sky and beautiful sunshine. The air was brisk with frost, and redstarts were singing from various tree-tops. I had a look at Hosking's hide but did not disturb the hen which was sitting. The cock flew past me with a flash of blue and with quick wing-beats disappeared.

As the first cotton wool of cumulus gathered in the sky, I made my way down to Loch Morlich. The four miles to the loch-side was the most delightful walk of my life. The wonder of bird-song; the gradual opening out of the high Cairngorms; and the glory of colour everywhere. It is beyond me adequately to des-cribe it: you must go there in May and see it for yourself.

At Loch Morlich I had a second breakfast, parked my ruck-sack—now quite light—and went bird-watching. In an old decrepit stump of a rotten tree a pair of crested tits had young. They allowed me to watch them, popping in and out the tiny nesting-hole at only a few feet distance. It is a lovely habit they have of shimmering their wings and raising the barred crest when excited. Siskins with a clamour of chirruping were feeding on a pine near by and I had good views of this bonny finch with the black face and lovely greenish-yellow plumage.

On the loch were five goosanders, two wigeon drakes, and mallard with young. A pair of greenshank skimmed the water, occasionally flashing a white rump which distinguished them from the commoner redshank. Going round the loch I was astonished at the variety of bird life. Of nests I saw two sand-pipers with eggs, one oyster-catcher, two of redstarts in deep holes in old trees, one meadow-pipit with cuckoo's egg, and, of course, blackie, thrush, hedge-sparrow, etc. But most interesting to me was a view of a family of crossbills at work amongst the pine cones. Side by side they were, the brilliant male as red as a bullfinch; the female as green as a greenfinch; and immature birds, brown as a hedge-sparrow and similarly striated. Once too, a flight of lesser redpolls passed over.

I had to run for my train. That night I arrived in Glasgow at nine-thirty. Just twelve hours later I was in the army.

15

The Rough Bounds of Knoydart

SOUTH and west of where the hill road from Tomdoun crosses the fourteen-hundred-foot shoulder of Creag a' Mhàim to Glen Shiel, lies the "Rough Bounds", an area of narrow sea lochs between steep hills and wild, seldom visited glens. In olden times the sea was the natural highway to these lochs of Morar, Nevis, and Hourn. Contact from inside was made by difficult hill paths that apparently baffled road engineers, and to this day they are the only means of communication. No other area in all Scotland is so bereft of "amenities" or so difficult of access. It was my intention to explore this vast unspoiled corner of western Scotland called Knoydart.

An examination of the map was the first essential. I would require food for at least a week, camping equipment, etc., so a good spot for a base-camp seemed the most likely beginning. The west end of Loch Quoich was most suitable, for the road to Kinloch Hourn—a dead end—would take me to a track leading to Kinloch Quoich. The next question was transport. Beyond Tomdoun, no information was available except that on certain days during the week a mail-car was reputed to call at Kinloch Hourn. I solved the problem by piling all my stuff on to my old bicycle, loading it on to the train, and getting off with it at Spean Bridge.

It was the last day of April when I wheeled my goods out of the station. The bike was as difficult to control as a bucking bronco, for I had such a load strapped on to the back of it that the front wheel had a tendency to become airborne. Nor did another load on my back help matters. I prayed that I might not get a puncture, and in a high wind and threatening rain pushed up Loch Lochy into Glen Garry.

Here my flagging spirits were invigorated by a blink of sun on the birches and a sparkle on the loch; chaffinches were singing and I heard my first cuckoo of the year. Low cloud enveloped the tops. Then I hit a bumpy road and at every jerk expected to get thrown, or even worse, a puncture. But luck was with me, and despite a fearful sliding and slipping I got to where the road petered out at Kinloch Quoich.

There was a house, and after a few words with the keeper I was invited into a little barn a few hundred yards away. It was better than camping on a night like this, and anyhow I was just in time for bed. I slept well that night, contented with the way things had worked out.

Rain battering down awoke me on the following morning. Snow lay everywhere above the two thousand feet level and this the first day of May! But an even greater setback was a visit from the keeper on the opposite side of the river.

"What will you be doing here?" he asked in an aggressive tone. He was a tall thin fellow, hostile and rather suspicious looking.

I said I hoped to climb a few of the surrounding hills.

"That's it," he said, "I feed the deer all winter and people like you come up and chase them all away. And when the gentlemen come, there is nothing whatever to shoot."

But for the keeper who had given me the freedom of his barn, I could see I would have been sent packing. I tried to reason with him, pointing out the obvious, that at this season of the year the deer wander in search of growing grass, and that my presence could have no effect on their usual habits. But he kept interrupting me and shaking his head angrily. I changed my tactics.

"Have you ever heard of Kenny MacKenzie of Wester Ross?" I asked him. He had. "Well, let me tell you something. Kenny MacKenzie is a friend of mine. I have stayed with him just to get some of his knowledge on the habits of deer. There is a man who knows more about the habits of red deer than any man in the county of Ross, and if he was here he would tell you that you are talking rot, absolute rot."

Carrying forward the bluff I told him I was an expert naturalist. What little I knew I made the most of, and as a result won the day. I had permission to climb on his precious hills. Actually, what the poor man was afraid of was losing his job, for it is a great crime to harbour strangers here. We became good friends eventually, but I was saddened to think that this man's natural impulses should be crushed almost completely by fear of losing his job.

At midday, as it does so often in the merry month, it cleared considerably so I set off for Sgùrr Gairich by a fine hill track that led to the shoulder. Two thousand feet of interesting climbing brought me to the top in time for a clearing as the mists rolled back. The Glen Finnan hills were revealed, shaded a beautiful blue and swept by fast-moving cloud shadows. Eastwards to Loch Garry and the south, gleams of sunshine lit the verdant country to rich greens, but the "Rough Bounds" that I so much wanted to see remained hidden. From all directions clouds were advancing on my peak, wiping out vast areas each second. The compass saw me back to the track, and as I got to the barn the rain lashed down.

Cumulus clouds floating over and among the snow-spattered peaks, gleaming wet slabs, and the foam of myriad mountain torrents sent my spirits soaring on the following sunny morning. As quickly as I could get off I was on Sgùrr Mór, the shapely peak immediately above me, and each upward step had a thrill in store. The whole wild tangle of mountainland unfolded, and its fierce peaks, deep glens, and lonely lochans were my dream come true. A golden plover sprang off its eggs at my feet, and near the top I came across the nest of a ptarmigan complete with seven eggs. Round and round the latter bird went, trailing its wings and scuffling over the ground like a rat, but I knew it had no broken wing but merely wanted to take my eye from its nest.

From Sgùrr Mór, the ridge runs over Sgorr Beag, An Eag, Sgorr nan Coireachan, and Garbh Chioch Mhór, culminating in the spike of Sgorr na Cìche that hangs 3,410 feet above the narrow head of the sea loch of Nevis. It was a great moment for me when I stood looking down into the loch after that great ridge wander, as satisfying as anyone could wish for.

For a long time I stayed up there watching the sun turn the Minch to silver and paint the purple I love on the Small Isles of Rùm, Eigg, and the edges of the Cuillin. East and south, huge gatherings of clouds blotted out the peaks one by one until I was surrounded by bad weather except to the far west. From a cloud-gap the sun shot a ray of light on to the very summit I was on. I was comfortably warm but now all around me veils of rain were falling. I felt that nature was paying me homage, but at last I had to go, and with deep regret plunged into the rain-drenched glen for the long walk home.

While there was some hope in the weather, it seemed to me a good time to get over to those outlandish peaks of Ladhar Bheinn, Meall Buidhe and Luinne Bheinn, that dominate the south shore of where Loch Hourn broadens out before joining the Sound of Sleat. There was a house at Barisdale Bay: if I could get accommodation there and a boat, I could perhaps traverse over Ben Screel into the bargain, and cross back over the hills to Kinloch Quoich. It was an ambitious undertaking but had a novel appeal. So, with lightly laden sack and wearing the lightest of clothes, I made the crossing of the pathless Glen Cosaidh to the woods of Glen Barisdale where low down I got a track that took me to the house set above the curve of the bay.

The keeper was friendly and quite pleased to put me up, but did not encourage the idea of climbing that night. Not wishing to upset him I went bird-watching by the sea pinks of this delightful shore. And there was plenty to see: oyster-catcher, ringed plover, dunlin, curlew, redshank, and out to sea were eider duck, common scoter, merganser, and red-throated diver. Meadow-pipit and rock-pipit were at their diving and singing, stonechat and wheatear chacked merrily, and from the rhododendrons came songs of blackbird and thrush, redbreast and hedge-sparrow.

But I did not expect my patience to be put to a three-day test, for it blew a storm for the next seventy-two hours. On the last day of it the keeper eyed the seas anxiously, wondering if he could safely cross to Arnisdale for bread and other provisions. A launch from Mallaig had been sheltering with us, and it was decided that the keeper should travel with his own little boat in tow and get a lift to the nearest point to Arnisdale, where he could change into his own craft; the launch would then proceed to Mallaig. I offered my services and was readily accepted.

All went well in that exhilarating sea of tossing spray until it came to changing boats. The problem was to wait for a wave to lift the small boat level with the big one and jump on before it disappeared into the trough a full ten feet down. I heard a cry of "now". I stepped on and went down as though I had stepped into space. The keeper landed in a heap beside me. While I tried to keep the boat head on to the waves he worked at the outboard motor.

We could not get it to do its duty, for as often as not the

propeller was whirling in the air where the boat had been thrown. I saw by the keeper's face that he was worried. But gradually through the rain, the blurred houses of the shore crept nearer, and under the lee of the land we were safe.

Proof that I have not exaggerated this sea is forthcoming when I say that for the first time during the whole year, winter included, the Mallaig mail-boat did not make the crossing, judging the sea to be too rough. Our journey was in vain. However, I have happy memories of the good lady at the wee post office who made us tea and let us sit at her cosy fireside while we waited for the sea to calm.

Against local advice, we set out on the return journey. Fighting a sea like this is like mountaineering on difficult ground. You have so little time to reflect on the "imminence of dissolution", a vision "that the hangman himself with all his paraphernalia of scaffold, gallows, and drop could hardly hope to excel", that you press on to the task in hand, in my case bailing furiously to win against increasing streams of green water. The keeper battled with the engine and kept the head of the boat where it should be. I envied the eider ducks so confidently riding the waves. No men ever set foot on land more gladly than we when at last we touched down in the bay.

Mist was low on the following morning but the air was still, birds were singing and I could see that the morning sun was winning the struggle. With high hopes, therefore, I climbed up on to Meall Buidhe, and the clouds rose with the widening view. A haze dimmed the isles pale blue, just a shade deeper than the sea. I was now between the two fiords of Nevis and Hourn and in a situation to appreciate the full beauty of these incomparable arms of the sea.

Over slabs of grey rock the ridge crossed to Luinne Bheinn, and here on its rocky top I had a comical encounter with a brood of ptarmigan. In little balls of yellow fluff they scattered over a huge slab. The mother gave the warning note and down they clapped, bills laid flat and bodies rigid. In this environment, of course, there was no protective concealment, but such was the discipline of instinct that although I peered at each in turn, not one moved. Meantime, the old bird was in a rare state, trailing its wings and moaning as it scudded back and forth at my feet, frantic because I was not paying it any attention. I retired to a short distance and watched. Nor had I long to wait. The mother gave a loud "cluck" and up popped every chick, running to her at once. In single file she led them away out of sight, a pretty platoon.

Now it meant a big drop from Luinne Bheinn to climb Ladhar Bheinn but it was early in the day and the visibility was improving. It was with keen anticipation, therefore, that I climbed up the rocky slopes of this most westerly of Scotland's three-thousand-foot mainland peaks. And what a wonderful peak it is, with a twin rock buttress that soars up from the corrie to near its pointed top.

Never did the glory of the west burst on me with such joyous impact than from up here. From Ardnamurchan to Torridon, and from Skye to the Outer Islands was the amazing panorama of mountain, loch, island, and sea, rich with the soft light of evening. How long I stayed I do not know, but as I came down the west ridge, all Loch Hourn blazed with gold and above it rose a peak of purest purple, Ben Screel; to-morrow I would tread its summit.

Sunrise on the morning was as vivid as the sunset preceding it and I knew the day would not be worth much. The keeper ferried me across the narrows of the loch, we said our good-byes, and round this natural rock garden of a coast I skirted to get on to Ben Screel.

Rain met me half-way up, and all I saw from the top was grey squalls of rain sweeping the Sound of Sleat and hosts of advancing clouds. All day it rained, but I heeded it not, for I had a long way to travel to get to Kinloch Quoich, first by a *bealach* of grim peat-hags, then scattered birches, then another wilderness of peat-hags until at last I was among the pines of Kinloch of Hourn. It was grand to breast that last rise Sgùrr a Chlaidheimh for the last lap over eighteen hundred-foot shoulders and see below me the loveliness of Loch Quoich and the friendly little barn. Tired but happy I crept into my sleeping-bag after a fine meal cooked over the Primus.

The days that followed were clear and warm. More provisions were forthcoming and I had good times climbing and bird-watching. Spidean Meallach and Gleourach was a fine expedition, but best of all was the traverse of two ideally situated little peaks, Sgùrr a' Mhorair and Am Bathaich. The sunset I saw over Rùm and the Cuillins is one of my best memories. It was an evening when visibility was limited only by the curvature of the earth. Lewis, Harris, the Sutherlandshire peaks and the Torridon mountains, the north-east face of Ben Nevis; all were crystal clear. Overpowering too were the tremendous ridges of Glen Shiel; the unique view of the Sgùrr of Eigg, and the aiguille-like spire of Sgùrr nan Gillean of Skye. I realized the full significance of the term "Rough Bounds" as I looked over the massive bulk of the thronging mountains from Sgùrr Mór to Ladhar Bheinn.

16

Torridon

It was March. I was tired of travelling; the weather was not inviting, but throughout the bombing, shelling and discomfort of soldiering I had consoled myself with the thought that when I got leave I would go to Torridon.

Torridon! What a flood of memories it evoked. I was a boy again, seeing for the first time the unsuspected wonders of a mountain bulkier than I had even thought existed—Liathach. I could see its twin curves, black as ink against moonlit skies, as it was that night we arrived in Glen Torridon after crossing the Coulin Pass in darkness. On a steep bank above the river was a little tent outside which a camp-fire was blazing. I could see myself at the fire and John contentedly smoking his pipe. Above us rose the long ridge of Beinn Eighe, pale in the moonlight. At our backs were the gnarled shadows of pine trees reaching up the hill-sides.

Often and often, as a youth in Glasgow, I had comforted myself with our wanderings; relived the rock-climb we did on Sgùrr Ruadh; did again that wonderful traverse of Liathach; seen the Atlantic glisten in silver from Ben Alligan; and viewed that tremendous panorama of wild peaks that is the reward of a good day on Slioch.

Now I had my longed-for leave, and here I was, reluctant to go. The imagination seemed a poor thing before the comforts of home. March is a treacherous month and notoriously unsettled. Also my mother was not at all keen on my going away. Rain and wind would be my portion. And the imagination stretched the glen to immense heights, down which monsoon rains poured, and the air was loud with the rush of cataracts and thrashing wind buffets. But I had written to say I was coming, so I steeled my waning resolution.

My luck started when I caught the late train and got enough of a compartment to sleep all the way to Inverness. There was no connection until midday but I stormed a goods train and thus got to Achnashellach well ahead of time. My rucksack I left at Achnasheen to go by mail-car.

What a morning! Frost rimed the trees and grasses and the paleness of sky betokened the glorious blue that followed. Up climbed the red sun but I had no thought of shepherd's warnings or the like. My eyes were on the peak of Fuar Tholl. A glittering frieze of snow topped it, making beautiful contrast against blue sky. Cutting the crags in an eight hundred foot sweep a fine snow gully led to the frieze. I resisted its temptations and amongst the pines of the River Lair I swung along carefree and happy. Tits were ringing their little bells from the trees and from the cascade on my left a wren was trilling its heart out. Already there was heat in the sun.

Soon I was on the col and ahead lay the desert greyness of Beinn Liath Mhór and Sgùrr Ruadh. The silvery sparkle of the burn led through pines below me to Loch Dhughaill and beyond it were the green hills that mass above Loch Monar, Maoile Lunndaidh being conspicuous. Far from trampling on a perfect memory as I had feared, I felt the most perfect kind of pleasure. A line of crags cleft by a deep gully promised a scramble, and a delightful climb on sound rock it proved to be.

But what a thrill it was to top the boulders and see the quartz ridges of Beinn Eighe and the spires and pinnacles of Liathach opening out at every step! The years slid away as I recaptured their magic. Far below was Loch Coire Lair flanked by the rock buttresses John and I had climbed so long ago. Over the fine ridge of my peak I went, quite dazzled by the sheen from sun-refracted snow and quartzite. Only the faintest breeze stirred a soft breath. I took my shirt off and basked contentedly.

From the last top I could see the tiny doll's houses of Annat bordering the blue of Loch Torridon. Straight for those houses I made. Ptarmigan creaked from their stones, revealing when they flew, that they were still dressed for the snows. Once an eagle flew over, soaring and flapping great wings black against the sky. By a reedy lochan I watched Liathach sculptured by the lowering sun; sculptured by dark cleaving gullies and picked out with rock ribs; all leading up to the shattered point which was the glowing top of the main peak, Spidean a' Choire Léith. All Glen Torridon was alight with rich colour as I strolled down to the village. Mrs. MacKenzie had a bath and an omelet of real eggs for me. I turned in to the house when the peaks were purple and the sea only a shadow.

The sound of the wind made me think the weather had changed when I wakened on the morning following, but over the loch was Ben Alligin, rose-tinted against the morning sky. Up the glen it was different. Dark clouds hid the peaks and were tossing in a way that suggested the sun was only having its hour. From Beinn Liath Mhór I had seen a steep snow gully on Meall á Chinn Dearg so I decided to go up there, for whatever the weather did, I would be promised a good climb.

My way lay over to Bealach na Lice and up this geological paradise I climbed; by long naked slabs of sandstone scored by deep grooves where in ages past the glaciers had scraped; and along natural terraces and remains of old moraines where three lochans, bare and windswept, lay. You do not need to be a geologist to appreciate that here you are on the most ancient floor in the whole world, the rocks breaking through the thin skin of earth in sandstone and quartzite tell their own story. Only the meadow-pipit, ptarmigan and eagle, mountain hare, fox and red deer, occupied the upper reaches beyond the trees. It seemed strange not to hear the cries of wading birds but they were at their winter haunts.

I went over broken rock to my snow gully and was soon hacking steps in its *névé* with my axe. Views from the top were restricted, so instead of lingering I glissaded on good snow down to Coire an Ruadh Staic. The climb on to the top of the peak, An Ruadh Staic, was first-class on rocks sound and steep with a plentiful supply of good holds. Views were improving now so I decided to extend my ramblings to include Ben Damh, especially as it had an interesting little knob of rock on it.

The climb was well worth it. Beinn Eighe and Liathach were clear, and westwards the sea lochs were a dim silver. This is where Beinn Liath Mhór shows off, for it is seen as a cone of delicate beauty from here. Down to the foot of Beinn na h-Eaglaise I went for the walk back by the Alt Coire Roil.

To come down from the naked tops to clustering pine trees and a deep rocky gorge down which an enormous waterfall tumbles to end in a rainbow, is surely nature's perfection. Below the defile of the gorge was the sea loch of Torridon, and rising

over it the peaks of Alligin and Dearg. All the variety of p↑
mountain form is here, tender and austere.

Down in the glen the tiny hands of horse chestnut were
emerging from their cuffs of crinkled bud. Daffodils were
blooming, and blackbirds and thrushes, hedge-sparrows and
robins mingled their songs. Mrs. MacKenzie's dinner deserves
a pæan of praise too. That night I would not have changed
places with any man alive. A *céilidh* in John the postman's
house just put the right finish to the day. They are kindly people
in this glen who know how to make a man at home.

A fresh morning with bright sunshine and lovely colour on
the sea and hills followed. Mrs. MacKenzie lent me her bicycle,
so I pedalled round to Coire Mhic Nobuill to where the track
skirts up the glen. Below Ben Alligin to where Ben Dearg rises
as a shapely peak scored with crags and by various little rock
problems I reached the top. This mountain has a fine summit
ridge and a dizzy little pinnacle that hangs over Loch á Coire
Mhoir.

Due north, by the blue lochs of Bheallaidh and Houigh and
the mountains of Bus Bheinn and Beinn an Eòin, were the
islands of Loch Maree and the familiar hills of Poolewe. Liathach, unfortunately, was buried in mist so that I was denied the
view of its spectacular north face I so much wanted to see, for
I had never forgotten my early impression of the descent of
Coire na Caime and the walk below its two miles of crags.

However, mist or no mist, I would climb it, for the day was
young and I was still fresh. Soon I was down among the fairy
mounds, sorting a way out amongst this tangle of moraine debris
that is the lower part of Liathach. Even as I climbed, it was
clearing, and there was the most marvellous effect of Coire
na Caime. Its northern projecting wall, over a thousand feet
of rock, was a silhouette. Purple shafts of sunlight poured
through gaps in between its pinnacles, and above it and behind
it, a fanshape of snow led up to the warm tinted edge of shattered
ridge which was the summit. Yet the whole effect was of perfect
symmetry, the central figure being the turret of Mullach an
Rathan.

Spidean a' Choire Léith was my peak. It was in mist, but a
scramble across bands of steep sandstone made a grand way of
arrival. From here the ridge to the west leads over tottering

pinnacles and sensational edges. The view down to Glen Torridon is an aerial view, unrestricted by any foreground slope: "Liathach, rising sheer, from river-bed to the sky", is perfect poetry on it.

Over its fingers of sandstone and quartz ridges I went to the Mullach itself. I was within six steps of the cairn when with a loud beating of wings up sprang an eagle. I leapt forward to see it and could have struck it down, so slow was it in getting away. But I was unprepared for a second one that almost touched me with its wing. I had a perfect view of its tawny neck, wicked hook of beak, and yellow, grasping talons. An unusual encounter, to say the least, with plenty of surprise on both sides.

All that remained now was a stroll over Sgorr a' Chadail and a descent to the bike for the ride home. I was hungry when I got in, but Mrs. MacKenzie soon put me right with a meal that included a cream-adorned trifle that was a work of art. And it tasted even better than it looked. That night I went to bed tired but happy.

It was dull next morning but I hankered after a climb up my old friend Beinn Eighe, at present wrapped in mist. Again I took the bike so that I could do a traverse from the east end. There was nothing to see. The mist got thicker and thicker as I climbed until all that could be seen was six feet or so of ridge. On top a fierce wind made weird noises amongst the pinnacles and numbed feet and fingers. Now and again I heard snow-buntings tinkling, a comforting sound in this loneliness of shifting scree and dripping rock.

At the peak west of Sgùrr Ban I struck south and was lucky to hit a snow-filled gully made for glissading. A swoop of nearly a thousand feet and I was soon on the road to be blown back to Annat on the east wind. Another *céilidh* with John and a few of the villagers passed the evening in true Highland style.

The morning brought with it sunshine again, and all the hills were sharp and clear except for odd wisps of cumulus drifting on the tops. The loch itself was calm and blue in contrast to the greens and browns of the shore and dun larches stretching up the hills to where heath and rock started. But I had decided it was my duty to go and see my old friends the MacRaes of Carn Mór. They had left their old home by Fionn Loch because life was insupportable with all the sons in the army, and were now installed in a wee cottage two miles from Achnasheen. It was a blow all the same, leaving a village where I had made so many new friends.

What a welcome I got at Druimdhu. Of course they did not know I was coming. Mrs. MacRae, beaming all over, shook my hand heartily, and then in came Alex and Callum, both on leave, so my luck was indeed in. Callum was cheerier than ever despite army .life. It was great to see Mary and Katy again, and even the dogs Crimson and Nessie were there, wagging their tails, Nessie grunting with pleasure.

Tea, a lot of talk, and some of Mrs. MacRae's famous bannocks, and we were united again. Crimson and I excused ourselves and climbed Fionn Bheinn. It was a long way from there but flightings of snipe, golden plover, curlews and grouse enlivened things and were a surprise considering the quiet of the Torridon mountains. Once on the snow Crimson had a great time and proved himself a mountaineer by glissading on his tummy down steepish slopes, rolling over on his back, and kicking his legs occasionally. Most mountaineers perform this sequence occasionally in the reverse direction but with less control over the proceedings than Crimson.

Fionn Bheinn is usually dismissed as an uninteresting mountain, so its steep north-east corrie overhung with snow cornices and broken by steep rock and snow slopes came as a surprise. Heavy hanging clouds lay over all the tops but I was able to recognize most of them. Most thrilling to me was Loch Fhada and the crags of Beinn Làir indicating that wild tangle of peaks of wilder Ross. Slioch was enormous, thrusting above huge shoulders, and once Liathach towered out of the mist like some tremendous cathedral. A pale light caused by the westering sun lit what could be seen of Glen Torridon. All the mystery of that fascinating glen was expressed for me by it. Loch Fannich was at my feet, a dark loch hemmed in by bare snow-topped peaks, each a beacon in my store of happy memories. We *céilidhed* well into the night on my return, a happy night as ever was.

All night it had rained but when I said my good-byes the sun was on the tops and the colourful clearness that follows rain bathed everything. How can I forget the splendours of silver bark on the birch against dark rocks and heather; wild glens gauzy with rain showers; and the blue of the Cairngorms, blue until the lifting clouds suddenly revealed snow-fields that had the sheen of satin over a thousand feet of their tops; and the stretching pines of the old Caledonian forest of Rotheimurchus reaching to the highest hill pass in all Britain. Great to see Glen Feshie again and watch wild duck slant in a whirling flock to plane down on a hill loch. All this from a railway train!

Yes, as on my arrival, the Highlands were showing me to the last, just how much they had. To think I had ever doubted coming up here. "Perpetual Youth"—that is what the mountains have to offer.

17

Glen Strathfarrar

FEBRUARY is not a good month for mountaineering, so when Charlie Downie and I decided to go up to Glen Strathfarrar —the most northerly of the three wild glens that reach westwards from Strath Glas—we knew we were likely to have a difficult time. The Scottish Mountaineering Club's *Western Highland Guide* says of it:

Owing to the scarcity of public accommodation in the district, the hills are, as a rule, rather difficult of access, and long drives are required in almost every case. For several of the hills west of Monar even driving is of little use.

Monar was the place we decided on for headquarters. The first setback came at Beauly when we heard that there was no mail-car available at Struy as we had been informed. Struy is at the entrance to the glen. A motor-cycle is used three days a week to deliver mail and food to the outlandish country which we wanted to explore, and no accommodation is available for luggage or bodies on that vehicle. So there was nothing for it but to hire a car from Beauly. This came after a telephone conversation, a long wait, and the repair of a puncture.

It was a beautiful morning, still and calm, with a delicate warble of bird song, the first I had heard that year. Robins and thrushes were the chief singers. A pointed snow-peak with the sunlight on it, in the direction we were going, raised the spirits high.

The ride through the Druim Pass, its black waters in wild spate tumbling through rocky bluffs and green twisted pines, with beyond, the snowy ridges disappearing into smoke-like clouds, was as fine an impression of Highland grandeur as I have ever had.

Then, after Struy, we got climbing by a bad road into wilder and wilder country, into the inevitable rain that has always been my portion in the neighbouring glens of Cannich and Affric. By a fierce gorge we came to a lovely little corner, steep with rocks

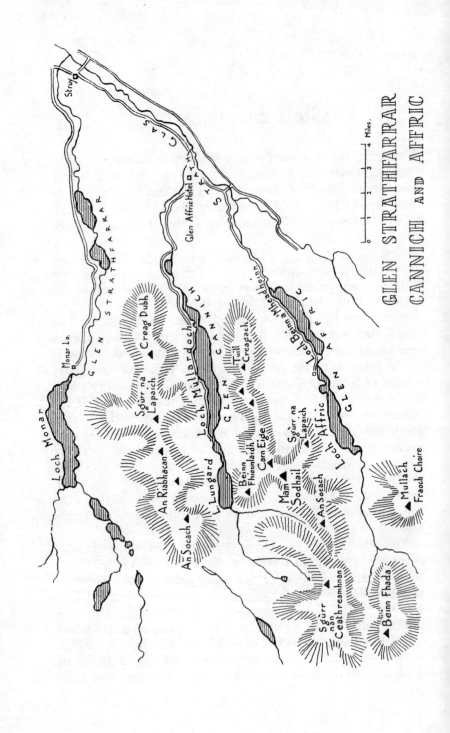

GLEN STRATHFARRAR
CANNICH AND AFFRIC

and woods, and edged by a loch, Loch Monar. The house where we were hoping to stay was perched on a green knoll.

It was much too beautiful a spot to get a second disappointment: the keeper's wife could not take us in. Now in planning this tour we had decided that we would carry sufficient gear to be self-supporting for at least three days. What we required now was more food and somewhere to shelter. There was a partly-furnished house we were invited to use, a store of firewood, and beds. The car-driver consented to take a ration card and get food sent up to us. The first problem was solved. We installed ourselves, had a meal, chopped up some wood, and went for a walk.

It was a bonny spot. There were blinks of sunshine to enliven things and glimpses of our peaks as the mists shifted on the snows. By a rocky hill-side and a path of pine needles we strolled, all the time accompanied by the "belling" of tits from the pines, and the "crar, crar" of hoodie crows. We had a fine view of an eagle being mobbed by the grey-coated gentry. It looked huge in comparison to the little fellows. In stately flaps it continued to quarter the hill-side, not heeding the attentions one whit.

Feeling at peace with the world we strolled back, lit the fire, and cooked ourselves a grand meal of soup and black puddings. We spent the evening with the keeper. He had just come in after eleven hours on the hill. The conversation was good and we received some instruction in the art of brose making, also meal and salt for the purpose. Brose is a kind of gruel made by simply adding water to some oatmeal seasoned with salt, sugar, and butter. Stir it up, leave it to steam for a few minutes and it is ready to serve. It certainly keeps the hunger away for a longer time than most foods.

We slept well that night and after a frugal breakfast of brose and half a slice of bread, set off for the hills in falling showers. The introduction was very beautiful due to spasms of sunshine lighting veils of rain and spanning the rocky jaws of the glen with a quivering rainbow. High up was a patch of blue sky and illumined against it the snows of the Lapaich ridges. And the perfect foreground was the torrent of the Garbh Uisge rushing in fierce cataract between rock walls and scattered pines.

But wild weather was piling up on the west wind, and as we

climbed into the corrie of Loch Toll a' Mhuic we had the last
glimpses of sun we were to have for some time. The snow, unfortunately, was in a deplorable condition and the rocks were not
much better because of streaming water. We reached the top
of our peak, Sgùrr na Fearstaig, by a straightforward plod for
the most part, and followed the corniced ridge over the grand
series of tops that leads to the most easterly peak, Sgùrr Ruadh.
The only views came from the latter peak, glimpses of Ben
Wyvis in sunlit brown, but the promise was not fulfilled. It was
disappointing to cross a ridge of fine peaks and to get nothing for
it but a buffeting from the wind. South took us to the glen for
the seven miles walk home.

Hunger made us force the pace and we talked as we walked
of what we would cook to make the most of our limited supplies.
But the kindly people of the house made our planning unneces-
sary. No sooner were we in than the boy of the house appeared
with two steaming urns of venison and potatoes. And the food
from Beauly had arrived. We felt very much at home at the
keeper's fireside that night.

The dawn chorus of the birds wakened me, robins predominating, and chaffinches doing their best to get beyond the first few
notes of their song. In dull weather we set off for Sgùrr na
Mhuice for an alleged great rock. We did find a rock but it
was not so big, four hundred feet perhaps, and it gave a fine
climb on sound rock with small clean holds. On top the weather
was wintry and we were glad to get down. In the glen it was
sunny and before we got back to the house the tops were clear.
We felt we had been cheated. It did not keep clear for long
though, which was balm to our injured feelings.

We were invited up to the keeper's for dinner and had a merry
night with this happy family. The keeper with his fund of good
stories and tales of hill days kept us going till well past midnight.
He had been on the hill practically every day since the previous
August, killing hinds to send away as food. Nor had he a word
to say against mountaineers. His versatility extended from shoe-
making—as fine shoes as I have ever seen—to an electric light
installation driven from the burn. This is what I call true educa-
tion in action.

Rain and wind was our portion in the night but at eleven a.m.
next day it cleared. The top of Sgùrr na Lapaich was revealed

and westward at the far end of the loch, a pointed peak supported
on knobbly rock shoulders, Bidean an Eòin Deirg. The latter
was the peak we were going to.

Packing up and cleaning the house was the next job; then to
get peats and wood to take up to the west end of Loch Monar by
boat, a gift from the keeper. Unfortunately these preparations
were not quite complete when we were told the boat was on the
point of leaving. A furious half-mile dash with all our stuff
loaded on a barrow, Charlie holding it on and myself pushing,
saw us to the boathouse, and to our relief, the boat. Almost like
a "flitting" we got aboard, and in showers of cold rain sailed up
to Strathmore at the head of the six-mile loch, as remote a spot
as could be found situated in the hills of Ross.

The keeper had promised us the use of a little hut he had at
this end of the loch and it proved a comfortable place complete
with beds and furniture. We man-hauled our loads up to it, got
a fire going and felt very snug indeed.

A cloudy morning but with blinks of sun after a wild, windy
night. We left for Sgùrr Choinnich which was situated in the
clouds. We found the top but got little else except a first-class
soaking on the way up and a good blow across the top. The
snow was in much better condition, and frosted grasses and ice
testified to lower temperatures. A compass course took us on to
the narrow ridge that rises in rocky steps to Sgùrr a' Chaorachan,
and borne on the wind, we ran across to Bidean an Eòin Deirg,
the fine peak we had admired yesterday. From the summit cairn,
tottering snow cornices overhung steep slopes that were the
supporting walls of a wild corrie.

Drenched to the skin we got home, ready for a change of
clothing and a meal. We spent the evening making soup, using
a tinned variety of stuffs, a bit of venison, and a couple of
spoonfuls of Bovril. It was a memorable soup. Enjoying dry
clothes and reading by the fire seemed the height of luxury
indeed.

The following day was hopeless for climbing: continuous
showers, the mountains leaden with clouds, and all the time
racing squalls of rain hurrying on the west wind. We lit a fire,
cooked breakfast, and played chess till lunch-time, when we
wandered out in search for firewood. That wild day I heard a
chaffinch trying its song and watched a cole-tit exploring a hole

in the shed. We got our wood, also some potatoes from the shepherd.

Then came the hurricane. Wind rose in the night and brought snow down to the thousand foot level. Despite it, we made up Maoile Lunndaidh. It was an exciting day, the clouds being thrashed open from time to time to reveal tremendous snow plumes streaming from the enormously high-looking peaks. The jostling from the gale and assault of a fury of hailstones were bad enough on the way up, but they were nothing to what was coming.

I have staggered across a few tops in my time—once on Ben Dorain in a wind that was recorded at 100 m.p.h. in Glasgow, when we crawled the length of the summit ridge and I was blown off my feet on the way down—but I do not remember any prolonged feeling of insecurity like that day on Lunndaidh. On our first top we had a wonderful glimpse of the Bidean. Cut off from the earth and trailing a gigantic snow-plume, its pointed summit could have been any height. A peculiar bluish tint on the snow contributed in no small way to its huge effect.

"This is the greatest day I have ever spent on a mountain," Charlie bawled in my ear. A strange thing, pleasure! We had one respite from the wind, at the great corrie of Fuar Tholl Mór, and we were privileged to look down its corniced depths to three inky lochans. A wild, beautiful corrie indeed, with good winter climbing in it. As we moved away from this lip the wind smote us again.

Lying flat and digging in with our axes to avoid a force that plucked at us like mighty hands; crawling, compass in hand and stiff with cold, we at last got to the other top. *En route* to it we had seen fair-sized stones, some as big as cricket balls, being lifted off the ground and carried through the air as though made of paper. We were afraid to stand up, and the effort of seeing was considerable owing to the blizzard of flying snow.

We came down by the east side to get into the lee of the mountain, crossing back to our original glen by an easy pass.

The shepherd with great consideration brought us a cooked meal as soon as we got in. That was a kindly action not to be forgotten. We were invited down for the evening also. That was a fine night. Father, son, and daughter made up the family and they were quite happy in this desolate spot. The young man, the shepherd himself, laughed enormously at any little turn of humour, holding up his hand and shaking his shoulders with mirth. His honest red face was a pleasure to look at, shining with good nature.

Outside, the storm grew wilder, .with flashes of lightning and low roars of thunder. The hail was a continuous rattle, and inside the little shed the noise of the gusts was frightening, each one cracking against it with a drumming noise that seemed to rock its foundations. The noise got worse and worse and sleep was impossible. Towards morning the intervals between gusts got longer, and although conditions were still fierce and much snow had fallen in the night, we deemed it feasible to attempt the hill crossing to Achnashellach. If we left it another day we were almost certain to be snowed in.

The twelve miles across was as tough a twelve as I have ever done. Deep drifts, fierce blizzards, the gale in our teeth, our heavy bags, and the trackless steeps of the *bealach* all made for gruelling work. We were thankful to get down to Gleann Fhiodhaig in the lee of the mountains. Our speed to that point was one mile per hour. It was lovely to descend effortlessly to Glen Carron and see green ground again. Above Achnashellach were the mighty tops of Fuar Tholl, Sgùrr Ruadh, and Beinn Liath Mhór which Charlie was seeing for the first time. He was duly impressed by these icy peaks.

In hail we got to the station for a brew of tea and the last of our soup, before the train left for Achnasheen. Two miles of snowy road to Druimdhu and it was *en route* there that we had our first accident. Charlie fell off the main road, disappearing into the darkness with an anguished cry. He had stepped aside to let a car pass and gone over the six-foot bank! As his landing was in deep snow, his chief damage was shock. Laughter seemed to be the cure.

We got the usual fine welcome from my old friends the MacRaes. It was worth such a beating from the weather to come back to my second home.

18

Applecross

Aｐｐｌｅｃｒｏｓｓ is the name given to the peninsula of Torridonian sandstone that forms a headland between the lochs of Carron and Torridon. There is no through route to Applecross. All the roads come to a dead end which perhaps explains why the district is threatened by mass evacuation. It was a district I had never been in, although often, when passing down the Kyle railway, I had admired the steep walls of its mountains. Perhaps it was because they lacked the magic height of three thousand feet, perhaps because of their inaccessibility. Anyway, it was not until the third stage of my demobilization leave that this deficiency was made good.

We were told, Charlie Downie and I, that a mail-car left Shieldag at nine a.m. each day, and as we were climbing in Torridon, the sensible idea seemed to rise early, tramp the seven miles round the coast, and catch the car. It was an ideal morning for early rising. The seventh of March, a perfect sunrise, the loch a flat calm mirroring the great snow-peaks, and the woods and moors prickly with brilliance.

Following the curving bays, in and out amongst the pines, we tramped, heavily laden but quite happy, stopping now and then to take a picture, or watch the little flocks of golden-eye ducks, black-throated divers, and red-breasted mergansers. Shieldag is a lovely little village which this frosty morning looked truly superb, the fishing nets hanging out to dry in front of the whitewashed houses.

Then came the snags. The mail-car had gone. We had been misinformed as to times. A telephone call to Kishorn elicited the information that no lodgings were to be had in the village of our hopes. This was a serious situation but not one for which we were unprepared. An obliging shopwoman gave us what we needed in the way of provisions, and unloading at her shop was a lorry which was about to go in the direction we wanted. Yes, we could have a lift to Tornamfreas. With a cardboard carton full of food, ice-axes, ropes, sleeping-bags, stove, etc., we clambered aboard for the exciting run to the head of Loch Kishorn. Exciting because of the glimpses into some of the wildest corries in all Scotland.

Our spirits were high. We had never imagined anything so fine. There was a house at Tornamfreas and we were promised the use of the barn. It was an unprepossessing accommodation, open slats of wood admitting wind and cold, but we were uninterested in personal comfort just then. We were anxious to get off to the hill.

What a mountain is Ben Bhan! We went into the eastern corries to look at the most formidable cliffs and towers in the whole district. In this great inner chamber, like two horseshoes separated from each other by a pinnacled ridge, we saw magnificent rock scenery. On our right, above a frozen lochan, was a rounded rock turret perhaps five hundred feet sheer. Behind it rose a steep arête as long again, rising to the very summit. A' Poite it is called. All the face left of the arête was an ice-fall, extending in a wall of rock and ice to a trio of towers that was the enclosing end of the horseshoe. This ridge of towers is known as A' Chioch, and the lowest is cleft by a narrow couloir up the whole length of its face which looked possible to us. We promised ourselves an attempt on it. With the sun shining, contrasting the rock, ice-falls, and corniced summit, the effect on this snowy mountain was spectacular indeed.

Under the turret of A' Poite we climbed, heavy going in deep soft snow, but giving views through rocky jaws to the greenery of the strath far below, and beyond that to the snow-peaks of Strathfarrar which had roughly handled us three weeks before.

Despite the lateness of the hour, I was optimistic enough to predict a route on the final arête of A' Poite, so we roped up and put it to the test. On difficult rock and insecure snow ledges we reached a long pitch of very steep and smooth sandstone. Charlie had no belay and a slip was not to be thought of; also it was time we were on the way down. In consequence of these factors, my attack was half-hearted, and so we were defeated within three hundred feet of the top. As far as possible we roped down, and just in time, for an incipient blizzard had blown up and the gloom of the night was descending. It was seven p.m. and dark when we got to the house.

Barns are useful places but bitterly cold in the month of March when you come in with wet clothes and have to sit around waiting for your food to cook. The constant vigilance required to ensure that the place does not catch fire is another drawback, not to mention the difficulty of producing food that is uncontaminated by an infiltration of hay. Luckily we were invited down to the house for a "warm", so what remained of the evening passed pleasantly.

I told the shepherd to give us a call at eight a.m. He did, and in doleful tones announced that the tops were in cloud and new snow lay on the ground. In the darkness of our loft we had only his word to rely on, so we lay till midday. To our astonishment when we rose we found that the sun was shining and only an odd bank of grey showed where snow had fallen. This shepherd prophesied nothing but grief to foolish people who climb hills in winter, so I have no doubt that he misrepresented the weather in the interest of our souls.

However, an off-day was due to us for we had been climbing steadily in Torridon for over a week. We went to Kishorn, intending to do some bird-watching *en route*. But this easy walk lasted until tea-time for we talked at length to everyone whom we met. Views over the loch to A' Chioch of Sgùrr na Chaorachan showed it to be a beautiful pillar of rock over a thousand feet high and shaped like twin barrels, one on top and one slightly behind the other. We hoped to make an attempt on it.

A miserable morning followed, with the hills in cloud and a west wind blowing the inevitable rain. We sat around getting colder and colder until at length we decided on a foray for digs. There was a ruin to be seen two miles off and, if it gave enough shelter and we could get a fire, we could go there. As we approached the place we noticed another house. From it a tweed-clad figure emerged and came towards us. He was a good-natured looking man and gave us a hearty greeting. We told him our story. "Come up to the house and I'll see what the wife can do for you," he said cheerily. Yes, the wife would take us in. "No one should be in a barn this weather." In no time tea was forthcoming and dry socks were forced on us. Our luck had turned.

Happily we strolled back to the barn, wheeling a bicycle to effect the "flitting". But poor Charlie had a shock in store for

him. Three telegrams awaited him, ordering him to report back
to his ship forthwith. His indefinite leave had come to an end.
So he left me and I did the "flitting" solo—not at all an easy job.

I knew what comfort was that night and was only sorry Charlie
could not share it. What grand people were these MacKenzies!
It was natural that this man should be a cousin of the late John
MacKenzie of Sconser, famous as the only native to climb the
Cuillin in the capacity of mountain guide.

The sky was dull and overcast but the tops were clear as I
made my way into Coire Chaorachan to inspect this crag of A'
Chioch. It is a fierce-looking place, not suitable for a solitary
man, and I contented myself with ascending the rocky edge of
the south wall of the corrie. From here the ridge bends in a half
circle and drops in a succession of pinnacles to A' Chioch. The
traverse of these pinnacles was far from easy owing to deep,
water-logged snow which had a tendency to avalanche. The
way to the Chioch itself was up a little rock rib to the top. Below
me was the whole face, a thousand feet down. A gale was blowing up here, so I was glad to glissade a gully, make a short
traverse to avoid a rock pitch, and find myself down.

Then came the kind of winter's day that you dream about:
frosty and sunny, with a haze that heightens the peaks and sends
a great stillness over everything. A day when "The curlew
whinnies wild", and even the stonechat tries its chipping song. I
went to Ben Bhan to see those wonderful corries again and this
time to reach its top.

The frost had bound the snow, and in a narrow gully I found
myself cutting steps in the best of stuff. A steep band of ice with
a bad take-off from an insecure stance called a halt, so I traversed
on to the right wall, and, after some difficult climbing on exposed
rocks, got into the gully. The exit over the cornice was a problem.

While climbing this gully I had a unique experience. I was
cutting a step when I caught a movement above me. Instinc-
tively, my head pressed to the snow and I dug in with the
point of the axe. But they were not falling stones. They
"swished" down the gully in a mad dive, wheeling out with
tinkling sounds when they reached the bottom—they were snow-
buntings having a frolic.

By this time the haze had thinned and it was clear and sunny
for thirty miles or so. Finer than any were the Torridon peaks,

their snows rather yellowish in tint, and Liathach and Beinn Eighe appeared as a succession of pointed peaks. Westward the Kyle was coppery, the indented coast and little islands black as ink. Raasay was clear, but the Skye hills were indistinct and of the Cuillin nothing was to be seen.

Over delicate cornices on good snow I traversed north, out over every corrie to the point above Loch Lundie, all of it above rock scenery exquisitely modelled with hanging ice and snow. Some of the gullies in these corries offered terrific problems to an iceman. It was good to stand above Loch Lundie and look across its blue water to the tiny houses of Shieldaig and the colourful shores of its sea loch, and beyond that again to the textured snows of Ben Alligin.

The cold, despite the sun, was bitter, and the return journey over the long summit quite fatiguing. Sunset was a quiet affair, but the tinted snows and calm sea lochs were very soothing to see. Dinner was waiting for me when I got in, for the keeper had been watching me through his telescope as I came along the summit skyline on the way home.

An overcast and windy morning followed. I set off for Meall Gorm up the Bealach na Ba, stopping *en route* to examine a huge boulder, the neighbouring portion of which is said to be at Gairloch, at least, so the keeper was informed by a pair of visiting geologists. How the forces of nature could remove two portions of a huge rock fragment so far apart is beyond me, but quite conceivable I suppose, if one could picture the enormous size of the glaciers which tore this wild country to its present form.

South, where the wind was coming from, dirty weather hid the hills, and before very long a blizzard was blowing. The pass with its gloomy crags and deep-scarred snow looked very inhospitable indeed and no place for a tourist. I pushed on with the ascent, choosing a gully with an adjoining rib of rock, so that if the snow was soft, I had an escape to the right on harder material. It was hopelessly windy and cold for rock-climbing so I contented myself with an odd scramble and some step kicking.

On top the mist was thick enough to call for the compass, and by its aid I followed the ridge down to the sea. This Meall Gorm is a fine little mountain, barrel-shaped like A' Chioch and presenting a continuous line of crags on its north-east side.

The weather cleared almost as soon as I touched down on the

shore, and by the time I reached the house the sun was shining full blast and the tops were looking their best. It was annoying not to get the celebrated view westwards to the isles but that is how the mountains treat their devotees sometimes.

That was my last climb in Applecross: next day saw me off again. I felt sorry to leave this house where the people had been so good to me but I was off to Skye where I wanted to see the Cuillin while the snow was on them.

19

Keepers and Keepering

My first brush with antagonistic keepers came early in life. It was a moonlight night when John MacNair and I arrived in Glen Torridon from over the Coulin Pass and pitched our tent on the overhanging bank of the river beneath Beinn Eighe. We were weary from pack-carrying but a fire of heather roots soon had a can of tea on the boil, and, with a candle going inside, our house was very snug. Everything was just as a perfect evening should be, when the sound of voices came to our ears and growling dogs were sniffing amongst us.

We were challenged to explain ourselves in a tone of angry authority, and before we could answer our tent was ransacked—for guns and fishing rods we were told when we protested. There were four of them, big ruffian-like fellows who were sure that they had caught somebody red-handed. As befitted the younger member of the party, I left the talking to John.

He explained that we had come over from Achnashellach and were spending our holiday camping and walking; that it was too late at night to think of asking permission to camp; and that if we were unwelcome we would take ourselves off in the morning.

"You are not fishing or shooting then?" "Have you a motor-car?" "Maybe you are expecting a motor-car?" Each keeper had a turn at questioning.

"Wait a minute," said the patient John, "we have no motor-car. We do not fish or shoot, but are just walking round as I have been doing for years."

"Were you ever up this way before?" said a voice.

"Yes," said John. "As a matter of fact I was at a wedding in the next village not long ago which you may remember. . . ."

That set them off. Did they remember!

"Remember this song?" asked John, and he broke into a Gaelic song, his voice full of the lilt of it. One by one they joined in.

"Dash it, I remember you singing it at the wedding. It's a grand voice you have."

Out came a bag of sweets with apologies that there was nothing stronger and more liquid in form. They had all been to the wedding and recalled with delight the hundred barrels of beer and fifty bottles of whisky. We finished up by singing Gaelic songs until the early hours of the morning. The forest was unlet that year, we were told, and there would be no objection to our climbing. We were treated thereafter as gentlemen.

. . . . .

Imagine the "wattest wat day in Lochaber" and a pair of misguided climbers coming up from Inverie on Loch Nevis, over Meall Bhuidhe and Luinne Bheinn, to traverse in long boggy miles the way to Kinloch Quoich. They were my friends Drummond Henderson and George Elliot, and their bedraggled hopes were buoyed by the promise of the little barn that had been so kindly placed at my disposal a fortnight before as described in another chapter.

Soaked to the skin and utterly weary by pack-carrying all the way, they tottered into Kinloch Quoich. They had sent parcels of food and clothing to the house and were anticipating with some relish dry clothes and a good meal. But there was no barn for them. The keeper who had done his best to prevent me from climbing flew into another of his rages. His precious deer had been disturbed, and feet other than the Laird's had despoiled the glen. They could go where they liked, he did not care, but there was no barn for them. That they were drenched to the skin, hungry, and shivering with cold did not matter. It was late at night and becoming dark in this inhospitable corner of Scotland. But for the intervention of the friendly keeper on the other side, the situation would have been grim indeed for them.

What was the explanation of this inhuman conduct? The Laird was expected on an early fishing trip. Such is the power of some Lairds. On another visit to the same spot, my friends found this keeper a different man: he treated them as old friends and could not do too much for them. The Laird was in London.

. . . . .

For three days I had not seen a human being, and it was with a keen sense of anticipation that I dropped off the wild moors of Sutherland to a little lodge situated on the edge of some peaks I wanted to climb. I had walked far across trackless country and I told myself that I would ask for shelter and food as a pleasant change from camping and my own company.

I knocked at the door of this out-of-the-way house. It was opened by a red-haired woman of sullen visage. I said I was walking and thought perhaps she might be able to supply me with a meal. Her, "No, there is nothing for you here", was the tone she might have used to a tramp whose visit was more than unwelcome. The door was closed in my face.

There was an outhouse not far off. The door was unfastened and the place would give shelter from the wind and rain. The shed was completely empty so I could not be doing any harm. I filled my pan with water, unpacked my stove, and was in the act of lighting it, when I saw an angry-faced man in tweeds and a deer-stalker cap advancing on me.

"What's this? You have no business here!" he shouted. "Come on outside! You can't come here doing as you like."

His manner struck me like a blow on the face. I said that I was only sheltering to keep myself dry and to get a little cover for the stove to keep out the wind.

"Stoves! Fires!" he shouted. "You come here disturbing the deer, walking where you like and spoiling the sport, breaking into houses . . ."

"I think you have said enough," I broke in. "This is not the sporting season, and as for fires, there is nothing to burn. Furthermore, I should have thought you would offer this kind of accommodation to a tramp—it is only an old shed. As for the country, it doesn't belong only to the Laird you know. A few million of us happen to be fighting for it right now."

"I am a soldier on leave," I went on, "and you tell me that I shouldn't be here. Where should I be?" Then I told him what I thought of people like himself, uncivil and impolite, interfering with other people's pleasure. He should be thankful to be tucked away in the hills and able to live a full life more or less undisturbed by war.

I had packed up my stove by now and lifted my bag to go when he stopped me.

"You'll be all right here," he said. "We have to be careful

with people up here, but I see I have made a mistake with you."
His tone was conciliatory. "Can I get you anything? Maybe
you would like an egg?" He brought me two.

We had a long talk and I was invited to stay for a night or
two any time that I cared to call again. I told him quite bluntly,
though, that there was no excuse for his inhospitality and abusive
language towards wayfarers.

.   .   .   .   .

There is an island in Scotland that typifies the whole evil of
the deer-forest system. It is a little island off the coast of Skye.
In one of Halliday Sutherland's books he tells of a young man
who wanted to leave the mail-steamer to visit the place. He was
prevented from doing so by the skipper of the boat, who
demanded a permit from the proprietor. The man had no
permit so he was not allowed to land.

At New Year 1945-6, some friends of mine decided to go to
this island on a little exploration trip. They hired a boat from
Soay, and, after five delightful days in fine summer-like weather,
it was time for them to leave. They had timed their climbing so
that they could depart on the mail-steamer which calls at the
island twice a week. The steamer came in to the bay but to get
to it they required a lift in the keeper's boat, the coast being too
difficult to let the steamer right in shore. The keeper refused to
have anything to do with them. They had got on to the island
without permission, so they could get off it without help.

This was a serious situation for my friends, involving the loss
of train connections, etc. They had to telephone to Mallaig, hire
a boat and wait for its reaching them. That hire cost them five
guineas and lots of trouble.

The owners of this island, I was told, visit the island for only
a week or two each year, yet a wonderful mountain range and
sea coast is closed to the public summer and winter. The keepers
act as policemen as well as preservers.

"You will always find with a Highland keeper," John told me
after the visitation of the Torridon keepers in the episode described in the opening of the chapter, "that he is suspicious of
you. Gain his confidence and he can't do enough for you." I
have had many years to put that truth to the test and some of
my most cherished friendships are with keepers.

I have told these stories, not to disparage a few individuals, but to try and present a serious matter in a true light. No class of men are more open-hearted than keepers. They have a tremendous knowledge of the hills and an understanding of the kind of people that climb them. The only thing that stands in the way of their complete hospitality is the deer-forest system which, happily, is on the decline in Scotland. I have not yet met the keeper who believes that the prosperity of the Highlands is dependent on the prosperity of the deer-forest.

It is the thought of eviction from their homes and the difficulty of obtaining alternative employment that makes the lot of the keeper arduous. The kind of welcome he can show to wayfarers depends on the kind of Laird he has: there are many good Lairds as well as bad, of course.

Recently I talked to a keeper on the subject in Glen Strathfarrar. "It all depends on the Laird," he said. "My man wouldn't care if the glen was thick with climbers, provided he got his sport on the hill. In fact, people wandering in a forest, even in the sporting season, can be a good thing. The deer have to go somewhere, and who knows that they won't come the way of a party that is just needing the luck."

I asked him what he thought of the future of the deer-forest system. "It will die," he said. "There is no heart for it nowadays. 'Gentlemen' are few, and the old comradeship between man and master is gone. The keeper is just a servant, not a very well-paid servant, and he has a lot to put up with. His heart is no longer in the work. The taxation is too heavy to maintain things in the old style anyway."

"Will that be a bad thing?" I asked.

"No, I don't think so," he said. "The deer forests have had their day. We want to encourage folks to the Highlands, not drive them away." That summed it up.

20

Solitary Mountaineering

I CAN see the brows of the purist lower and hear him mutter, "Even if this blighter does do so much solitary climbing, there is no reason why he should give folk a lot of funny ideas by talking about it. Set a bad example, etc., etc." The charge up to a point is justifiable, but I am unrepentant. If, on the other hand, some inexperienced enthusiast gets himself killed, however indirectly, through me, I shall be sorry that I ever put pen to paper.

It takes time to get used to solitary climbing, but the heady drink, once the palate is seasoned to it, has a flavour like no other. The senses I think, are sharpened, there is a heightened appreciation of beauty, a feeling of closeness to nature, and there is no other personality and its impact to bring you down to earth. Up there, the world is all yours.

Solitary climbing was forced on me. This is not an excuse but a fact. As a schoolboy, the Campsie Fells, ten miles from Glasgow, lured me. I was not at all interested in football or the usual games, and no friends of mine were sufficiently keen on the hills to walk the ten miles, or speculate the few coppers for the bus. So I walked it by myself. And thus began what became a weekly pilgrimage to "the mountains", for they were mountains to me.

Exactly when I first turned my attention to the face of rock three hundred feet high that is part of the hill-side above Lennoxtown, I do not know. But I remember encouraging, by a lot of fine words, a couple of lads to come out and sample it with me. As they were of an athletic turn, I expected them to follow me up the route I had discovered on the face. To my astonishment they funked it at a hundred feet, and one of them was actually in tears, begging me to get him down. After that I was regarded as something of a queer fellow—which surprised me to say the least!

Now, Arrochar and its famous Alps was only half a crown on

the bus, half fare, so one Sunday at eight-thirty a.m. I left on
Link Line's bus, armed with map and compass, and wearing a
pair of tacked boots. It was a beautiful day and I climbed the
Cobbler to glory in its views of Loch Long and Loch Lomond
and the mountain land north that I was determined to know.

Half a crown was a lot of money to me, but as often as I could
raise the money—and I sold wooden boxes for firewood to raise
it—I was up Loch Lomond-side or at Arrochar.

Then came a day when I saw a pair of roped climbers, the first
real mountaineers I had seen. They were climbing a deep
cleft on Ben Narnain, and breathlessly I watched them perform
the feat of climbing it. So this was real rock-climbing! When
they were well out of sight I started up it, shaky at first and
thoroughly windy before I was half-way up. My legs shook so
badly I thought I would never reach the grass at the foot of the
climb.

For a week that climb was on my mind. The very next Sunday
saw me on Narnain again. I got up it, wriggling through a cave
of jammed boulders to get out on the summit. Yes, it was the
"jammed block chimney", and I felt as proud as though I had
just topped the Matterhorn.

That was the beginning of a fetish for rock-climbing. I
scoured the familiar Campsie crags for new climbs and soon I
had my "Arrowhead Route", "Chimney Route", etc.—jargon
culled from climbing literature I had been reading and which my
imagination adapted to routes of my own.

Torridon and Skye and an introduction to real rock-climbing
took me away from the Campsies, and it was not until I had been
in Skye a second time that I went back to the fells where I had
served my apprenticeship. To my amazement, the climbs
horrified me, and never in my whole life have I been more
terror-stricken than on the direct route of my so-called "Arrowhead". There was a two-hundred-foot drop below, and eighty
feet of nightmare climbing had landed me on slender footholds
of rotten rock with one crumbling handhold for support. How I
made the delicate movement that gave me steep grass holds I
will never know, for I was in a cold sweat of fear.

As an inexperienced youngster, I had been climbing on these
suicide rocks week-end after week-end, by routes equally hairy,
quite unconscious of their potential danger. The moral of the

story is obvious. I had no judgment and consequently did not recognize the difference between difficulty and danger. To me, the Lennoxtown crags were rocks and I had climbed them, but I had no right to, as I understood all too well in the light of my subsequent experience. There lies the folly for the inexperienced in solitary climbing.

Rocks are rocks to young fellows struck with mountain fever, and, companions or no, they will venture on the nearest crags. It is this novitiate period in solitary climbing that is most dangerous, as recent accidents prove. It is my belief that once a man has found the measure of his skill and acquired judgment through climbing with men more experienced than himself, he is safe on rock, with or without the moral support of a well-belayed rope. And he will always keep well within his capabilities. Accidents are rare amongst solitary wanderers of experience—indeed I can think of only one in the sixteen years I have been climbing. Having to depend absolutely on oneself develops unusual care and attention to details such as time and equipment, route-finding, etc.

Not that I advocate solitary climbing. In my time I have climbed solo the great face of Sròn na Cìche in the Cuillin, and have a vivid recollection of clinging on to the west route, a pair of boots dangling round my neck as I negotiated the difficult little mantelshelf so sensationally set four hundred feet above the screes. Another recollection comes to me, of streaming wet rocks looming out of mist, and of myself edging my way up the direct route on the Eastern Buttress. And an exciting race with darkness across the eastern half of the "Girdle Traverse". Descent, with no doubled rope, of the "Tearlach-Dubh-Gap", on a wintry day that struck a chill to the heart as well as the hands.

. These things are not to be recommended. There is little to be said for them, considering the abundance of more suitable things for a solitary man. Of course I can make the excuse that it was lack of suitable companions that drove me to it. So it was, but that does not excuse me entirely. The fact is, I was selfish. I was pleasing myself before considering others, the people who find the body and carry it to its last rest. That is the ultimate objection to unjustifiable danger as found on the routes I have admitted climbing.

The late A. F. Mummery said that it is the pioneering of new routes that is most satisfying to the mountaineer. The solitary climber of proved experience and skill, confident in his resources, has something of that satisfaction, for his approach is the approach of a pilgrim seeking a special delight which is beyond the grasp of gregarious minds.

But the height of mountaineering enjoyment to a solitary man is not found in doing difficult rock-climbing. It should be kept within reasonable bounds so that it is a carefree business with no more risk in it than can be tackled with confidence. There are plenty of steep easy rocks in Scotland if rocks must be climbed, and this is the kind of thing which gives highest enjoyment. The chief pleasure is not the measure of climbing difficulty, but to be amongst the hills.

Winter climbing is a different proposition. I have done a lot of it and I do not recommend it for a solo climber. All the work devolves on one man, and in deep snow or icy conditions it is very exhausting work. Furthermore, unlike summer climbing, constant vigilance is necessary, even on simple places.

For example, on a traverse over the Cuillin ridge in icy conditions, there are few places where a slip would not be fatal owing to the tremendous steepness of the *névé* slopes and iced rocks. With two climbers, one could safeguard the other all the time. The strain on a solo climber takes all the fun away and makes a grim affair of this traverse.

Even on simple mountains conditions can be quite ferocious, as I discovered when climbing the featureless peak of Moruisg above Glen Carron. This normally grassy mountain was as slippery as an icy road, calling for extreme care, broken limbs being a likely consequence of a heavy fall.

The only occasion that I have ever hurt myself was when climbing solo under conditions of snow and ice. It happened in the Cuillin. I tell the story as a warning. I had traversed over from Sgùrr na Banachdaich to Sgùrr a' Mhadaidh under very bad conditions. On the ridge, ice was on the rocks with soft snow piled on top of it, and in the gullies and open slopes was real snow-ice, *névé*, with a loose covering of soft snow. There was no fun at all in the work, it was much too dangerous, and I was glad when I retraced my steps to the top of An Dorus for a glissade down to the corrie.

The snow in this steep gap was hummocky and like ice. Lower

down I could see patches of lighter coloured snow which indicated a variable surface. I let myself go. The ridged surface retarded that gliding motion so essential to good glissading. It also separated my feet. I was going fairly fast and had just taken the weight off my axe when I hit a bad patch of soft snow. My feet stopped but my body went on. The axe was wrenched from my hand and I went careering down the slope, head first and on the flat of my back. It was a fearful swoop, made unpleasant in the extreme by the certain knowledge that I must strike something. I tried to get into a sitting position but I was going too fast to do anything. My shoulder acted as buffer to the first rock I met and all but knocked me out. However, I managed to stop myself in the check of the collision.

I reviewed the damage. A brand-new Grenfell jacket had been ripped right across, and my right arm was more or less useless. My shoulder was throbbing with pain and altogether I felt pretty weak. However, I recovered the axe, returned to the house, and next day saw me in Broadford for an X-ray. I had torn some shoulder muscles and ruined a climbing holiday.

That is the kind of thing that could happen to anyone, solo or in company. But what would have happened had I been unable to get back to the house? Search-parties, trouble to the local inhabitants, discomfort and even danger to people unused to the more technical side of mountaineering.

That is the final argument against solo climbing in winter, when the difficulties and dangers are unpredictable and absolutely different from anything met with in summer.

Epilogue

Scenery, even the wildest which is really enjoyable derives half its charm from the occult sense of human life and social forms moulded upon it.

LESLIE STEVEN

IN this little book of mine there has been much exultation over wild places, a halo of pleasure when I have been able to find country remote from human contacts. But equally, you will notice, I have always been glad to find people—an odd family here and there that still lingers when all others have vanished, leaving only rickles of stones and green turf to mark their going.

There was one assumption common to all the friends I made in these wild places, but it was some time before its significance sank into my uncritical mind. The assumption was that the land was emptying; that it was the natural thing for their sons and daughters to leave home in their 'teens and find employment where it was to be had; in the town working in factories, in the Police Force, the railway, or in one of the professions.

The story was always the same. There was no future in the Highlands. Sheep-farming was a heart-breaking business owing to poor prices. Bad weather and foreign competition ruled out arable farming. Surplus milk could not be disposed of owing to lack of transport. And as keepering was only for the few, inevitably the land emptied; a way of life had been outlived, or was well on the way to it. Fishing where it used to be good was hopeless owing to illegal trawling, and often and often catches of herrings, when they were caught, had to be thrown back into the sea.

Even to keep a croft the crofter had to have an income outside it, either the old-age pension, most usual in the Highlands and Islands, or seasonable work of some kind that provided enough to make ends meet. Many of the Island piers were in a deplorable state, and boat services consequently impaired. But the Government, which was later to spend several millions a day on war, could not do anything about it.

137

The imposition of super-tax caused the sporting gentry to suffer too. Forests went unlet, and the dependent Highlander had to suffer also, since his way of life was founded on theirs. At this, the time of the Spanish War, the columns of every northern newspaper were overflowing with advertisements from eligible men seeking employment, all with the same story to tell. It was times like these that made some keepers forget their humanity and turn wet and weary wayfarers away from their doors; for they had jobs to lose.

Then, just before the war, came a proposal for a hydro-electric power scheme to generate electricity for a carbide factory vital to the manufacture of explosives. It was to be a private concern run for profit, and if it had gone through, would have affected some of the finest Scottish scenery as well as invaded the sporting sanctuary of Knoydart. The proposal was rejected, and I remember at the time being glad of it, for I was anxious to keep the Highlands unspoiled as I knew them.

But since then, and after some six years of war, I can see things more clearly. One thing that stares me in the face is this: many of the old houses where I knew friendly faces are now empty. The families I knew have at last found life insupportable, and the mountains seem the bleaker for their passing. And over all the Highlands this is happening.

It requires no great insight to see that if the young people go away, and the old people die, there is no one left to carry on. That artificial desolation which I have exulted in, creeping year by year beyond the zones originally devastated by the "clearances" fills me with dismay. I am old enough now to see that too much of Scotland conforms to my youthful specification.

So the problem is, how can we keep the youth of the Highlands in the Highlands? If the war has done no other good it has shown that Scotland's tremendous resources must be developed. At last money is not all powerful; goods and services, the real money, are more important. So Scotland is to have vast water-power schemes and an eighth of its surface planted with timber. Millions of trees will be grown and the power of the glens harnessed to build up this much battered land of Britain.

What will Scotland get out of it? If the Government keep faith we shall get new ways of life for Highland men and women; ways of life that make these fine people more than destitute crofters and lackeys to the well-to-do. Inevitably new towns will arise and new villages develop as the army of workers grows and grows.

It is estimated that more people will be employed in forestry than in the coal mines. The benefit to Scottish culture of this flood of life will be enormous. Into the bargain the subsidiary industries of water-power and timber will be considerable. This seems to me a much better solution than mere development of the tourist or sporting industry.

In the wild places, instead of grouse moors or deer forests given over to a few weeks' sport in the year, and housing a few keepers, we shall have, we hope, national parks timbered on their lower slopes, the glens cradling the villages, but all the upper mountainland free to the wanderer. No doubt the sportsman will fit into the scheme of things, but in his right place, not that of a god. And I am certain there will be plenty of Scotland as untamed as it is now, for ours is a gigantic mountainland. This is, in my opinion, the only alternative to a depopulated High-lands. The question of the Islands is a more difficult one and more linked in its solution, perhaps, with agriculture or cattle rearing.

Much beauty can be created by the growing of trees, and already the Forestry Commission have shown what can be done in places like Glen Shiel and Ben More. In forestry, particularly, we have a means of keeping the best type of man in the country in his traditional way of life—a life close to the hills and centred amongst them.

Some lines of Neil Munro's come to mind:

> Scotland! Scotland! little we're due ye'
> Poor employ and skim-milk board.
> But youth's a cream that maun be paid for,
> We got it reamin', so here's the sword.

We shall see if we can do better than that in the future.

Thirty-six Years On

In my mail recently was a letter from that most energetic of Scottish Munroists, Hamish Brown, suggesting to me I should try to get this book of mine republished. 'Your *Highland Days*,' he writes, 'has a great feeling of a different (kindlier?) world: pre-hydro, pre-forestry, pre-mobs—which, with its youthful enthusiasm, scores its song.'

By coincidence, just before this letter came I was talking about the old days of Scottish mountaineering with a climber of my own vintage and it threw up some interesting thoughts.

One was that if my father had been a climber he would have been rubbing shoulders with men like Naismith, Raeburn, Professor Norman Collie, Douglas, Ling, and many another hallowed name, including Munro himself.

My father would have been twelve years old when the Observatory Ridge on Ben Nevis was climbed for the first time, just six years after the Crowberry Ridge was conquered by an English party in 1896. The Highlands were new and all the great classic climbs were still awaiting exploration by its first generation of gentleman mountaineers.

The early journals of the Scottish Mountaineering Club capture the excitement of a time when the topography of our little-known mountains was still being unravelled, especially in the Cuillin of Skye, An Teallach, Ben Nevis and Glencoe. As knowledge accumulated, the data was gathered into 'Guidebook Sections' for easy reference to the various mountain regions.

A 'General Guide' to the Scottish hills had been in print for ten years when I began in 1931. The last section of my now dog-eared copy was a list of all the 3000ft. tops compiled and revised by Sir Hugh T. Munro, with page after page ticked off as I climbed them, and my dates alongside. I see that I had climbed 306 tops by the time war broke out in 1939. Other sections of the book deal with geology, meteorology, botany, birdlife, and details of where to find the best rock and snow climbing. The successor to this, *The Scottish Highlands*, written by W.H. Murray for the Scottish Mountaineering Trust in 1976, shows what a long way we have travelled in sixty years.

Working folk like me had to make do with the gentler hills near Glasgow in the unsophisticated days of the early thirties when Glencoe was a far off place accessible only on long weekends when shops were closed on Monday holidays. Our training ground was the Campsies, the Kilpatrick's, the Trossachs, the Arrochar Alps and the Loch Lomond bens. Come the month of May however, horizons would widen as Sunday excursions began running on the West Highland Line to Fort William, bringing Crianlarich and The Bridge of Orchy hills within day range. That cheap-fare train was like a mountaineering club meet of climbers, and it was there I met many of the men who are my friends today.

The teenager who was me didn't seek to understand his time. He was too caught up in it. I was quite unaware that the men I was meeting belonged to a new type of climber. The climbers I had read about in the Scottish Mountaineering Club journals were professional men. We were working class, less well-educated and certainly less sophisticated than the men who had inspired us by their writings. I was too busy finding my own joys, on the crest of the Cuillin, in the wilds of Knoydart, in the heart of the Cairngorms, even to think of such spin-offs as 'character training' or educational values obtained from reading maps and planning trips.

It certainly never occurred to me that there was much in the way of danger on the hills. After all, the greatest crags in Scotland had been climbed, summer and winter, for all of forty years before there was one fatal accident. Raeburn, doyen of early climbers, had been chosen for the very first expedition to Mount Everest. Collie died peacefully of old age in Skye, and in his old age repeated his own classic route on Sgurr Alasdair. Only thirty-nine years had elapsed between Collie's first ascent of the Cioch and my own, but it seemed an eternity to me at the time. In fact less was known about Skye than the fashionable European Alps when Collie came to the Cuillin, fell in love with them, and retired to live out the remainder of his life at Sligachan.

Collie's generation laid some excellent traditions, the most valuable being that the mountain is more important than the route. How attitudes have changed! Climbing has become a technical sport requiring absolute dedication and training to keep in the forefront. To reach the highest standards you have to climb more and maybe enjoy it less. I prefer the older mountain philosophy as expressed by the late Dr Tom Longstaff who, replying to a letter from Bill Murray when we were in the Garwal Himalaya in 1950, answered thus: 'Just travel is the thing. Number your red letter days by your camps, not summits (no *time* there). Enjoy—and for always, as you can thro' concentration.'

I think that quotation from Longstaff expresses an eternal value behind mountaineering. Murray has made the point often enough that it is relaxation after intense action which brings the most intense joy. I know from my own knowledge how a testing experience, come through safely, brings exhilaration. All of us want to prove ourselves. New equipment, improved techniques, have opened marvellous new opportunities for mountain exploration on what were thought to be impossible mountain walls at home and abroad.

Strangely enough, better equipment and safety aids have not made the mountains safer for the more ordinary climber. Hamish MacInnes has said that the chief deficiency of most people who get into trouble on the hills today is lack of basic mountaineering experience. Or, put it another way, not enough time has been spent walking and scrambling over hills and ridges at all heights and seasons.

The Cuillin Ridge is not quite so narrow as the hair of one's head, or as slippery as an eel of the river as the Cuillin legend tells us. But you have to tread warily and preserve vigilance at all times if you wish to survive. And this is the essence of mountaineering, the cultivation of an alert and perpetual awareness, especially on comparatively easy ground where a slip has killed many a highly skilled and experienced man.

But these are debunking days with a blasé approach to classic climbs which makes the early literature of Scottish mountaineering read like the work of anxious fuddy-duddies. Born into today's scene and attitudes, with present opportunities for leisure, I believe I could reach a higher technical standard in four seasons than I have reached in forty. Yet I doubt if my life would have been enriched by it. Prof. Collie thought the Scottish hills, and the Cuillin of Skye in particular, the most perfect of all ranges on which he had climbed, for quality of rock and beauty of form born of the mists. After a fair experience of the greater ranges of the world I am able to share his point of view.

Indeed I think my travels abroad, from Greenland to the Himalaya, made me see Scottish hills in a way that I hadn't done before, and appreciate the marvellous variety of scene and perfection of its small scale, changing so enchantingly with the seasons. Even a low island like Iona has the feel of a mountain experience when you go scrambling on the rocks of Dun I or scramble along the coast to the Spouting Cave. The rocky Hebrides are mountains submerged in the sea except for their tops.

One accidental thing I am grateful for is that I had no one to take me to the hills, show me the ropes, ease the way. I was led to them by having a passion for snow that still persists. In Springburn, the highest part of Glasgow, I could see the Highland peaks sparkling white while the daffodils were blooming in the cemetery which our house overlooked. The nearest hills were the Campsies and it was there I first tasted the joys of rock climbing, by forcing a way up three tiers of crumbling basalt above Lennoxtown. From that experience I began reading about Scottish mountains in the few books available on the subject in our public library.

The Cobbler seemed to be the place to go, half-a-crown on the bus—half fare, for at sixteen I was small for my age. I went with a younger boy, made short work of it, crossed over to Beinn Narnain and saw my very first pair of roped rock climbers in action on the Jam Block Chimney. I couldn't get them out of my mind, and the following week I went back there alone and with wildly beating heart started up the deep-cut rent in the cliff, gaining confidence with every move and arriving on top in a state of elation. All that was missing was a companion to share it.

But one was coming along, a red-haired lad by the name of Matt Forrester who shared my interest, was a loner like me, but a much bolder rock climber. It was with him I mopped up the Munros, and were he alive today he would shake his head with disbelief at the enormous patience of helmeted climbers festooned with equipment who can spend the whole day occupying climbs that we did together in nailed boots in the 1930s in a couple of hours, the Crowberry Direct for one.

This leads me to the conclusion that slow climbers like these are tackling routes that are too hard for them. Indeed it is my contention that although climbing standards have risen phenomenally above anything my generation could have envisaged, the average standard of competence has not moved appreciably since the thirties and forties.

The big take-off in climbing popularity was in the 1950s, after the climbing of Everest, a period which coincided with a rise in motor-car ownership, a rapid growth in the establishment of Outdoor Centres, and an emphasis on mountaineering by the armed forces. At the same time we had the RAF Mountain Rescue Service to combat the high accident rate from this continuing popularity, then the establishment of the local Mountain Rescue Teams, helped today by trained dog-handlers.

Anyone can have an accident. I've had a few of them, twice due to standing glissades which went wrong and should not have been undertaken. The first was after climbing the Y Gully on Cruach Ardrain on an icy day when, coming down from the summit, I suggested glissading it to the fork beyond which I knew to be rockily dangerous.

I went fast and well, too well, for I was unable to brake hard enough to stop, and shot over the fork to take a severe battering which could have killed me. I got away with a bruising which kept me off work for a week, but I got down off the hill under my own steam. The second occasion was during my demobilisation leave from the army, in February 1946, after an alpine ridge traverse from Sgurr Dearg to Sgurr a' Mhaidaidh, step-cutting all the way. That marvellous day ended with me glissading from the An Dorus gap, losing my axe as I went head over heels on ice and in the out-of-control slide struck a rock with my shoulder as I shot down head-first. Again I got down on my own feet, and Ewan MacRae of Glen Brittle House kindly accompanied me back to Glasgow after a visit to Broadford Hospital for an X-ray. No bones were broken, but the muscle had been torn off my shoulder and took a long time to heal. I spent the inactive period typing *Highland Days* which I had written while in the army.

Then seven years later there was the February accident on Stob Ghabhar when dangerous wind-slab caused us to abandon the famous couloir but not the climb, although we should have done, for the weather had worsened to incipient blizzard and our main wish was to get down. However, being fairly close to the top I decided to continue up the very steep slope leading to the invisible summit.

It all happened very suddenly. One moment I was kicking into the snow and pulling up on my dug-in axe, and the next I was tumbling over and over in the air. A mighty jerk was the rope breaking as one after another of my three companions were plucked off. We were lucky not to be buried alive, and to escape with injuries that enabled us to descend the long way round the mountain. Only a very early start saved us from being benighted. Injuries sustained were twisted ankles, a badly bruised back and skin torn from the face, broken ribs and a fractured patella. Only one of our party of four was unhurt.

Out of action from February until the end of May 1953, I was then in Glencoe and about to set off for the East Face of Aonach Dubh with Len Lovat when Tom MacKinnon burst into the hut and told us the great news that Everest had been climbed. I didn't know Len all that well then, but in the next seventeen years of accident-free climbing we were to have some great days on hard climbs before our evening of reckoning on Ben A'n when, for the first time, I was carried off a mountain.

I had led a very hard pitch with an overhanging start to the left of the normal classic route known as the Last Eighty. Len had made the first ascent two years before, and I had repeated it once since then. On this third ascent I was pleased I'd got up it so easily and didn't worry unduly about the fact that our shorter rope didn't enable me to reach the good anchorage I had used before. After all, Len is a much better climber than I am, and I'd never known him to make a false move.

So I was not well placed to hold a fall. I kept the rope fairly loose, for the first twenty feet of delicate moving needs fine balance and I wanted to be ready for the next hard move, rounding the overhang. Then I felt a tug at the rope which became a jerk. I held for a moment, then I went soaring into space, green hill and blue sky whirling. Len, falling backwards, saw me go over him like a sky diver and knew what to expect. As he hit the heather ledge he was in a sitting position when the jerk came on him. Digging in his boots he slowed the pace and managed to hook the rope round a rock.

Now he had to tie me to the rock, release himself, and climb down to where I hung unconscious. He was unhurt except for scratches, and he tells me I came to in a short time but seemed unable to comprehend what he was saying. All he knew was that I was in great pain and that I was shivering.

The time was 9.30 p.m. He told me, 'For God's sake don't take off that rope. I'll be back as quick as I can with a rescue party.'

The pain was such that I had to do something, get the weight off my chest on to my knees. The pain in my ribs made me gasp for breath and my back was in agony. The moon had risen and my teeth were chattering uncontrollably when I heard the voices of the rescuers at 1 a.m. Len had summoned climbing friends from Glasgow who had picked up a stretcher and two men from the Lomond Rescue Team.

Dr Jim Kerr, a ski-ing friend, administered morphine and his words about the state of my injuries were reassuring. At 4.30 a.m. I was in Stirling Infirmary. The damages were a squashed and chipped vertebra, a cracked hip and fractured ribs. It was November before I climbed again. Len explained how his fall had come about. He had made the big stretch to the tiny hold for the vital balancing move, and it snapped off in his hand.

I feel a very lucky man to be climbing, for my back was close to being broken and is so squashed that I am told I had better not have another accident to it. What I remember most vividly are the painful months when it was impossible to find a comfortable sleeping position, and the slow business of learning to walk again. So many people helped, nurses, doctors and friends.

I blame myself entirely for the accident. I should not have allowed Len to take-off on the climb without a good anchorage for holding him in case of a slip. The fact that I didn't expect a climber of Len's calibre to fall is no excuse. Fortunately he suffered no physical damage, but neither of us has climbed so confidently since.

The moral of the tale is, enjoy your climbing, observe the rules, play safe if your aim is the art of mountaineering. Rock athletics is a different sport, but one which will vitally affect the future of mountaineering by opening up unclimbed walls on great mountains of the world. A new dawn has broken.